Wall Street Versus Main Street

Understanding Why The System Is Broken

By John F. Ince

Published by:

The Serendigity Publishing Group

Email: info@serendigity.com

ISBN-13: 978-1468034318

ISBN-10: 1468034316

Version 1.1

To join with others concerned about general issues
raised in this book visit:
www.WSVMS.net

To order additional copies of this book visit:
www. WSVMS.com

To read John F. Ince's blog visit: www.JohnInce.com

To follow *John F. Ince* on Twitter visit:
http://twitter.com/johnince

For additional information or for discounts on bulk orders of this book
email: Info@WSVMS.com

THE ISSUE WHICH HAS SWEPT DOWN THE CENTURIES AND WHICH WILL HAVE TO BE FOUGHT SOONER OR LATER IS THE PEOPLE VERSUS THE BANKS.

- LORD ACTON

Acknowledgements

Writing this book will not have been possible without the support, input, ideas and insight from the following people: Chris Anderson, Author and Editor of *Wired Magazine*; Marc Andreessen, Internet Entrepreneur and Investor; Peter Barnes, Author, Capitalism 3.0; Robert Sheer, Columnist; Robert Johnson, Kenneth Larsen; Wayne Baker, Author, *Achieving Success Through Social Capital*; William Baue, *Sustainability Investment News*; Ellen Brown, Author: *The Web of Debt*; Leslie Berlin, Blogger; Tim Beyers; Richard Cashin, Managing Partner, One Equity Partners; Adam Cherier, Filmmaker and Book Editor; Clifford Cobb, co-author of *If the GDP is Up, Why is America Down?*; Marc Dangeard, Founder, Entrepreneur Commons; Liana DeBare, *The San Francisco Chronicle*; Joe Dominguez, Co-author, *Your Money or Your Life*; Jed Emerson, Uruhu Capital; James Fallows, National Editor, *The Atlantic Monthly*; Niall Ferguson, Author and HBS Professor; Steve Fraser, Writer; Edward Hadas - Editor, *Fortune Magazine*; Donald Gogel, Managing Partner, Clayton, Dubilier & Rice, Inc.; Paul Glover, Founder, Ithaca Hours; Thomas H. Greco, Jr. Author, *The End of Money and the Future of Civilization* William Greider, Author, *Secrets of the Temple: How the Federal Reserve Runs the Country*; Paul Haller, Teacher of "The Dharma of Money" at The San Francisco Zen Center; Ted Halstead, Founder, New America Foundation and co-author of *If the GDP is Up, Why is America Down? in The Atlantic in October 1995*; Charles Handy, *Harvard Business Review,* Arianna Huffington, Blogger, *The Huffington Post*; Carla Javits, President, REDF; Simon Johnson, Former Chief Economist, IMF; James Kouzes, Chair Emeritus of Tom Peters Company; Paul Krugman Economist; Bob Ivry, *Bloomberg*; John Kemp, Author of *U.S. & UK on Brink of Debt Disaster*; Mark Knoller, *CBS News*; Paul Lamb, Principal of Man on a Mission Consulting, Tim Leberecht, CNET News - Matter/Anti-Matter; Matt Lawlor, CEO, Online Resources; Bernard Lietaer, Author, *The Future of Money*; Michael Linton, *Local Exchange Trading Systems*; Lou Michaels, Author, *The Rainmaker, Thinking Outside the Box*; William R. Neil, Writer; Floyd Norris, Financial Columnist, *The New York Times*; Mark Pittman, *Bloomberg*; Tom Raum, Washington Office of the Associated Press, Mark Scott, Writer for *Business Week*; Howard Rheingold, Author, *The Future of Money*; Joseph Stiglitz, Nobel Prize-winning economist; Will Thompson, Thompson Doorman; Andy Tobias, Author; Nick Turse Blogger ; George Soros, Author and Investor; Joseph Stiglitz, Economist and Nobel Laureate

Table of Contents

Part I - The Education of a Banker

Part II - The Awakening of a Banker

Other Books by John F. Ince

MAIN STREET VERSUS WALL STREET: TRANSFORMING RAW ANGER INTO PURPOSEFUL ACTION - The System is broken, but how do we fix it? Capitalism is in the midst of an identity crisis. This book shows how Main Street can fight back against Wall Street level the playing field in the game of capitalism.

COMMON CENTS: NEW MONEY VS OLD MONEY AND THE NEXT AMERICAN REVOLUTION - Our world finds itself on the brink of an unprecedented crisis of an epic proportions, distinguished by the fact that so many sectors of society are simultaneously feeling its wrath. By decentralizing and democratizing the money and banking system we can revitalize our economy and usher in a new wave of wealth creation. All it takes is to apply modern technology to the task of innovating and modernizing an antiquated money and banking system that was first designed over 100 years ago.

MEANINGFUL MONEY: INNOVATION AT THE INTERSECTION OF MEANING, MONEY AND MARKETS - The root cause of our crises lies nowhere else but in our modes of thinking and these modes have become so deeply ingrained into our thinking. There is a revolution at work beneath the radar and it's all about rethinking the nature of money and the power it has over our lives. It goes by different names: social capital, social enterprise, impact investing, venture philanthropy, slow money and it's helping us to see a new way of imagining the most powerful tool ever created by humans: money.

THE HIGH GROUND THAT THE PROTESTERS SEIZED IS NOT AN ARCHIPELAGO OF PARKS IN AMERICA, BUT THE NATIONAL AGENDA. THE MOVEMENT HAS PLANTED ECONOMIC INEQUALITY ON THE NATION'S CONSCIOUSNESS, AND IT WILL BE DIFFICULT FOR ANY MAYOR OR POLICE FORCE

TO DISLODGE IT.

... THE STATISTIC THAT TAKES MY BREATH AWAY IS THIS: THE TOP 1 PERCENT OF AMERICANS POSSESS A GREATER NET WORTH THAN THE ENTIRE BOTTOM 90 PERCENT, ACCORDING TO AN ANALYSIS BY THE ECONOMIC POLICY INSTITUTE.

... THE SOLUTION TO THESE INEQUITIES AND INJUSTICES IS NOT SO MUCH SETTING UP TENTS AT BITS OF REAL ESTATE HERE OR THERE, BUT A RELENTLESS FOCUS ON THE COSTS OF INEQUALITY. SO AS WE MOVE INTO AN ELECTION YEAR, I'M HOPING THAT THE MOVEMENT WILL CONTINUE TO MORPH INTO: OCCUPY THE AGENDA.

- NICHOLAS D. KRISTOF

Part 1

The Education of a Banker

What is "The System?"

While an undergraduate at Harvard in the late sixties, I lived in an student house that achieved a reputation as a hotbed of radical activity during the campus protests. One of those activists was Senator's son by the name of Al Gore. Gore had to keep a low profile during the rallies, because his father was in a tight re-election battle in conservative Tennessee and Al's activities had become an issue in the campaign. In effect his father's handlers had asked Al to muzzle his mouth so that his father wouldn't suffer PR fallout. It was my first glimpse of how the system can force people to compromise their convictions.

During the student protests, I was fascinated by popular unrest as an instrument of systemic change. I attended teach ins, rallies and mass meetings, because I found the logic of the protests both exciting and compelling. Although I was raised the son of a conservative Wall Street banker, I found the logic of the protests compelling. The rhetoric was focused on the war in Vietnam, but it also involved a questioning of the system that had lead us into the war. Back then, very few of us students understood the system or how it really works, though we more than happy to rail against it. The strategy for bringing down the system was to use a sledgehammer of public protest. That's what the 60's "revolution" was all about. Somehow, by taking over buildings and organizing rallies, those who ran the system would cave into student demands, abdicate their throne of power and a better system would

prevail. With the benefit of hindsight, it's clear that the student's bravado was naive. But the passion behind the rhetoric was real, and its real again today in the form of The Occupy Movement.

Many of those ensconced in positions of power seem more human to me than to most people. I saw them when they were testing out their beliefs and their worldview was just taking shape.

When I was at Harvard Business School, I was a proctor in Harvard's freshman dorms when Ben Bernanke, now chairman of the Fed, entered as a freshman. He had come to the same font of learning as did John G. Roberts, who would live nearby in another Harvard house. Roberts is now Chief Justice of the Supreme Court. A few years later, Barack Obama studied at Harvard Law School and after classes used to play basketball in Hemenway gym, where I would play nearly every afternoon after classes. Mitt Romney later attended Harvard Business School across the river, just a few years after I received my MBA there. Living in such close proximity to those who today represent the system I know that the system is neither monolithic nor static. It fills me with hope that those of us now on the outside looking in, can change that system. Later in my career I worked on Wall Street with Chase Manhattan Bank until I soured on Wall Street and left to become a reporter with Fortune Magazine where I got another inside perspective on how the system works. Before we can change the system its inner workings must be fully

understood. What is the system? Who really controls the system?

What motivates these people. That's what this book is about – understanding the system and then working to change that system.

Actually those of us living on the metaphorical Main Street have a lot more control and power over the system, than we realize. We have a choice where we spend, deposit and invest our money. Yes,, "The System" is deeply embedded in institutional and inertial structure and propelled by levels of self-interest that are deeply ingrained in our culture. Changing the system will require not only support from within the system, but also coordinated and determined effort from outside – and that process of changing minds has already begun on the streets with the the beginning of The Occupy Movement.

The Essence of Wall Street's Strategy

I had my first real awareness the dynamics of "Wall Street" and its profound power holds over our lives in the 1980s when I was working in the real estate group of Chase Manhattan Bank on Wall Street. The economy was in trouble and the energy crisis had hit with vengeance. Interest rates had soared to 20%, as the economy tanked and defaults soared. Banks all across the country had dramatically cut back lending. Gas lines formed across the country. With an insider's view of the extent of the problems, I could see where we were headed, and I no longer wanted to be a part of the problem.

It was a turbulent time to be working on Wall Street. I found myself sitting in boardrooms lined with anxious bankers acting like predators, picking clean the carcasses of once high flying real estate companies. New York City was on the verge of defaulting on its municipal bonds. To bolster the morale of us bankers, David Rockefeller had a series of open meetings, where he would discuss the ongoing negotiations of Chase with New York City and Congress over the prospect of a Federal bailout. Chase and Citibank owned a huge share of New York's City's bonds and stood to lose billions if the City defaulted, potentially destabilizing the entire financial system. There was tension everywhere you turned.

Yet, I was surprised at David Rockefeller's composure during those meetings. He was a calm amidst the storm of widespread panic in the financial markets. It was only years later that I came to realize how he could be so calm – he knew that the system was functioning exactly as it was designed. Chase, which had taken imprudent risks in its real estate and municipal loans, would ultimately be

bailed out by the government. Sound familiar?

David Rockefeller knew this would happen. At the time I thought this crisis was an isolated instance of the government acting, in a state of crisis, to rescue the system from collapse. Since then I have come to see that these periodic spasms of the financial markets are entirely predictable. It is also predictable that in a state of crisis, the government will act to rescue the banks that caused the problems by taking on too much risk. The Congressional bailout bill was part of a larger pattern which would be repeated. It had rescued Penn Central and Lockheed in 1970. Later they would rescue Chrysler, Commonwealth Bank of Detroit, First Pennsylvania Bank, Continental Illinois and others. Then of course there was the savings and loan crisis in the late eighties and Long Term Capital Management in 1998, the bailout of Mexico and of course, the bailout bill of 2008, each instance rescuing a financial system that had come perilously close to collapse and required federal intervention.

This is how the system works. It's all part of the design of the system. It's reliable. It's hugely profitable for those on the inside, working on Wall Street. It's unfair to those on the outside, living on Main Street.

As The World Crumbles: The ECB Spins, FED Smirks, And US Banks Pillage

You can't gauge say, what happens if Goldman Sachs bets $20 billion in leveraged credit default swaps against Greece, and offsets them (partially) with JPM Chase which bets $20 billion, and offsets that with Bank of America, and then MF Global (oops) and then.....you see where I'm going with this. We're doomed if even their board games don't come close to mimicking the real situation in Europe, or in the US, yet they supply funds to banks torpedoing local populations with impunity. These central entities also don't bother to examine (or notice) the intermingled effect of leveraged derivatives and debt transactions per country; which is why no amount of funding from the ECB, or any other body, will be able to stay ahead of the hot money racing in and out of various countries. It's not about inflation - it's about the speed, leverage, and daring of capital flow, that has its own power to select winners and losers. It's not the 'inherent' weakness of national economies that a few years ago were doing fine, that's hurting the euro. It's the external bets on their success, failure, or economic capitulation running the show. Similarly, the US economy was doing much better before banks starting leveraging the hell out of our subprime market through a series of toxic, fraudulent, assets.

- Nomi Prins, Author

Privatizing Gain and Socializing Losses

Chase Manhattan Bank, back then as today, had placed big bets on risky real estate companies, both through the Chase REIT (Real Estate Investment Trust) and through the banks real estate department. During the heady days of the bubble buildup, Chase was reaping handsome rewards. They had loaned money, too often with inadequate analysis, because the interest rates they applied made those loans hugely profitable. Several of those loans went to a high flying resort developed called Sea Pines Company. Sea Pines, run by a visionary ex-lawyer named Charles Fraser who had bought up huge tracts of land on Hilton Head Island, Kiawah Island, Amelia Island, in Puerto Rico and several other choice spots throughout the Southeast of the United States. Sea Pines had ambitious plans for developing all these properties, building golf courses, tennis centers and tracts upon tracts of condos and homes for the affluent. Their plans were sexy and banks were throwing money at Sea Pines. Sea Pines became the top recruiter at Harvard Business School, hiring ten graduates that year. I was one of those recruits and became the right hand man of the COO of Sea Pines, an ex bible salesman, who had a gift for gab.

Working near the center or power of Sea Pines I had an insider's look at all the companies plans and projections. I began to feel queasy. The numbers didn't compute. There just weren't enough high income earners in the Southeast to support sales of all the homes and condos that were on the drawing board. I hired a market research firm to substantial my suspicions and presented the study to the President and the CEO in a tense private meeting. I could do this because a few weeks earlier I had told them I was going to leave the company. They were in denial about the

reality of the figures. Two years later Sea Pines was bankrupt and most of their loans were in default. By then I was on the other side of the lending equation working for Chase Manhattan trying to workout those loans. Chase eventually had to seek bailouts from the government to preserve the stability of the financial system. Chase was "too big to fail." This is how the system works. Banks privatize gain and socialize losses, with taxpayers picking up the tab.

Financial institutions take the risk and reap the rewards during good times. Taxpayers pay the bill during bad times. This is the way the system was designed – the very same system that David Rockefeller's banking predecessors had created almost 100 years ago at a secretive meeting on Jekyll Island off the coast of Georgia in 1913. Those bankers, representing 40% of the world's wealth, developed the blueprint for our financial system in their own self interest. Almost 100 years later, it's still working the way it was designed, benefitting banks that are "too big to fail," at the expense of taxpayers.

Understanding The System

The thought of rethinking the "The System" is one of those mental exercises that tends to make our brains seize up. Why is that? All kinds of systems govern various aspects of our society and our lives. What is a system if not a set of contracts, a set of technologies and a set of shared understandings? All these can be changed. All these can be renegotiated. All of these can be rethought.

For example I'm a basketball fan and during the recent NBA lockout and subsequent negotiations I got really confused by that back and forth of proposals. There was the simple revenue split, but then there were all the other rules regarding

 salary caps, amnesty clauses and on and on. When the lockout was all over I suddenly realized that basically what they had done was rethink the system. They had a set of rules that governed the contracts that determined how much the players were to be paid and how much money the owners were going to make. When one side (the owners) made a determination that the system was broken, they essentially issued a demand that the system be changed. They wanted different rules to divvy up who made how much. One can make all sorts of arguments as to who came out better in the new system, but that's not the point. The point was that the system could be changed.

So it is with the systems that govern capitalism. One side … call it Main Street has come to the conclusion that the system is really one sided in the favor of Wall Street and the result is economic injustice in the system of capitalism. But what are the rules that tilts the system in favor of Wall Street and can those rules be changed? Well, yes, they can … but first we've got to understand those rules and how they work to the favor of Wall Street.

A Watershed Moment in Wall Street's History

The seed for this book was planted over two years ago, when I stumbled upon an article on Bloomberg.com that described a watershed moment in the Wall Street history.

BLACKSTONE CO-FOUNDERS TO GET $2.33 BILLION IN IPO

JUNE 11, 2007, (BLOOMBERG) -- STEPHEN SCHWARZMAN AND PETER G. PETERSON, WHO STARTED BLACKSTONE GROUP LP TWO DECADES AGO WITH $400,000, STAND TO COLLECT A COMBINED $2.33 BILLION FROM THE LARGEST INITIAL PUBLIC OFFERING BY A LEVERAGED BUYOUT FIRM. THE 60-YEAR-OLD SCHWARZMAN WILL RECEIVE $449.2 MILLION FOR SELLING SOME OF HIS HOLDINGS, LEAVING HIM WITH A 24 PERCENT STAKE, NEW YORK-BASED BLACKSTONE SAID TODAY IN A FILING WITH THE U.S. SECURITIES AND EXCHANGE COMMISSION. PETERSON, 80, WHO'S RETIRING NEXT YEAR, WILL GET $1.88 BILLION AND RETAIN 4 PERCENT OF THE COMPANY. BLACKSTONE, MANAGER OF THE WORLD'S SECOND-LARGEST BUYOUT FUND, IS GOING PUBLIC AFTER SPENDING $199 BILLION ON ACQUISITIONS SINCE ITS FOUNDING IN 1985. THE OFFERING WILL PROVIDE SCHWARZMAN AND PETERSON WITH A BONANZA DWARFING WHAT GOLDMAN SACHS GROUP INC.'S PARTNERS MADE IN THAT FIRM'S INITIAL SALE. NOT EVEN GOOGLE INC.'S FOUNDERS REAPED AS MUCH IN THEIR IPO AS SCHWARZMAN WILL IN BLACKSTONE'S.... J. TOMILSON HILL, 58, THE VICE CHAIRMAN WHO HEADS THE COMPANY'S HEDGE-FUND UNIT, WILL OWN 1.6 PERCENT OF THE SHARES VALUED AT $535.4 MILLION, AFTER RECEIVING $22.1 MILLION. HE WAS PAID $45.6 MILLION IN 2006.

BY ELIZABETH HESTER AND JASON KELLY

Why should this particular news item have hit me so? Quite frankly, it really pissed me off. Why so angry? We often read news of Wall Street financiers or corporate executives who get obscene bonanzas and bonuses, but the news generally slides by us, as we move onto other things that we deem more important and immediate. This was different. This was more outrageous. This one stuck with me. This was personal. I know how these guys operate. I had experienced the influences that affect their world view and rejected many of those influences in my life. Suddenly the injustice of the Wall Street's domination of our economic system had a face to it.

$500 Million in One Haul

The Blackstone's IPO stood out as a defining event in the frothy explosion of Wall Street excesses– a period of financial prolificacy fueled by irresponsible risk taking and reckless use of debt. The Blacksone IPO set a new standard of excess in an economic system gone badly awry. It was the biggest U.S. IPO in five years and Stephen Schwarzman's outrageous financial bonanza clocked in at $7.5 billion. Blackstone instantly became a lightning rod for public outcry and questioning of "the system." Something was deeply wrong with the world of finance and the way our economy distributes wealth.

Tom Hill, who netted over $500 million from the Blackstone IPO, and I were suite mates at Harvard Business School. Steve Schwarzman was one year ahead of us at HBS. Just a few years before, I had interviewed Pete Peterson for my documentary, TIME-BOMB; America's Debt Crises Causes, Consequences and Solutions.

Where do they get their power? How is Wall Street's influence is created and consolidated? In other words, we need to understand how the system works. This is what this book is about. It breaks the Game of Capitalism into its component parts and analysis the advantages given by the system.

What are these people? [1] Steve Schwarzman was a year behind George W. Bush at Yale and both were members of the Skull and Bones society. After Yale, both then went on to Harvard Business School. Schwartzman graduated from HBS in 1972, a few years ahead of Bush and one year ahead of me. Schwarzman began his career in financial services at the now defunct, Lehman Brothers, where he reached the rank of managing director at age 31. He eventually became the head of Lehman Brothers' global mergers and acquisitions team. In 1985, Schwarzman and his partner Peter Peterson started Blackstone, which originally focused on mergers and acquisitions. In 2008, Wikipedia listed Schwarzman's net worth somewhere north of $8 billion. He was ranked by Forbes as the 53rd-richest person in America in 2008. On 13 February, 2007, Schwarzman celebrated his 60th birthday at the Armory on Park Avenue. Here's a clip from the New Yorker article, THE BIRTHDAY PARTY: How Stephen Schwarzman became private equity's designated villain by James B. Stewart.

---

[1] http://en.wikipedia.org/wiki/Stephen_A._Schwarzman

THE BIRTHDAY PARTY

HOW STEPHEN SCHWARZMAN BECAME WALL STREET'S DESIGNATED VILLAIN

FEB 11, 2008 (THE NEW YORKER) -- SCHWARZMAN HAS MADE HIMSELF AN EASY TARGET FOR CRITICS OF WALL STREET GREED AND CONSPICUOUS CONSUMPTION. HE LIVES IN SPLENDOR IN MANHATTAN, AND HE HAS AN EXPANDING COLLECTION OF TROPHY RESIDENCES THAT ARE LAVISH EVEN BY THE CURRENT STANDARDS OF WALL STREET. IN MAY, 2000, SCHWARZMAN PAID $37 MILLION—REPORTEDLY A RECORD SUM AT THE TIME FOR A MANHATTAN CO-OP—FOR A THIRTY-FIVE-ROOM TRIPLEX ON PARK AVENUE THAT WAS ONCE OWNED BY JOHN D. ROCKEFELLER, JR. IN 2003, HE PAID $20.5 MILLION FOR FOUR WINDS, THE FORMER E. F. HUTTON ESTATE IN FLORIDA, WHICH OCCUPIES A CHOICE SPIT OF LAND BETWEEN THE OCEAN AND THE INTRACOASTAL WATERWAY. DESIGNED BY THE PALM BEACH ARCHITECT MAURICE FATIO, THE THIRTEEN-THOUSAND-SQUARE-FOOT, BRITISH-COLONIAL-STYLE ESTATE WAS A DESIGNATED HISTORIC LANDMARK; LOCAL RESIDENTS WERE STARTLED WHEN SCHWARZMAN HAD THE HOUSE RAZED. ... IN 2006, HE PAID $34 MILLION FOR A FEDERAL-STYLE HOUSE, ON EIGHT ACRES ON MECOX BAY, IN THE HAMPTONS, THAT WAS PREVIOUSLY OWNED BY THE VANDERBILT HEIR CARTER BURDEN.... SCHWARZMAN ALSO OWNS A COASTAL ESTATE IN SAINT-TROPEZ AND A BEACHFRONT PROPERTY IN JAMAICA. HE TYPICALLY SPENDS SUMMER WEEKENDS AND AUGUST IN EAST HAMPTON; JULY IN SAINT-TROPEZ; AND WINTER WEEKENDS IN PALM BEACH. HIS CHILDREN USE THE HOUSE IN JAMAICA; HE RARELY GOES THERE. THE FIVE PROPERTIES AND THEIR RENOVATIONS APPEAR TO HAVE COST SCHWARZMAN AT LEAST A HUNDRED AND TWENTY-FIVE MILLION DOLLARS. "I LOVE HOUSES," HE TOLD ME RECENTLY. "I'M NOT SURE WHY." ... THE SCALE OF [HIS 60TH BIRTHDAY] PARTY DISAPPOINTED NO ONE. PART OF THE CAVERNOUS PARK AVENUE ARMORY WAS TRANSFORMED INTO A LARGE-SCALE REPLICA OF THE SCHWARZMANS' MANHATTAN APARTMENT BY PHILIP BALOUN, THE PARTY PLANNER WHO DESIGNED THE PRINCE CHARLES GALA AT LINCOLN CENTER. REPLICAS OF SCHWARZMAN'S ART COLLECTION WERE MOUNTED ON THE WALLS, INCLUDING, AT THE ENTRANCE, A FULL-LENGTH PORTRAIT OF HIM BY ANDREW FESTING, THE PRESIDENT OF THE ROYAL SOCIETY OF PORTRAIT PAINTERS. DINNER WAS SERVED IN A FAUX NIGHT-CLUB SETTING, WITH ORCHIDS AND PALM TREES. GUESTS DINED ON LOBSTER, FILET MIGNON, AND BAKED ALASKA, AND WERE OFFERED AN ARRAY OF EXPENSIVE WINES. (SCHWARZMAN HIMSELF DOESN'T DRINK.) THE COMEDIAN MARTIN SHORT WAS THE M.C.; HE POKED FUN AT HIS SHORT, RICH HOST. THE COMPOSER-PIANIST MARVIN HAMLISCH PLAYED A NUMBER FROM "A CHORUS LINE." PATTI LaBELLE SANG A SONG WRITTEN FOR SCHWARZMAN, AND ROD STEWART SANG A MEDLEY OF HIS HITS, FOR A REPORTED FEE OF A MILLION DOLLARS.

BY JAMES B. STEWART: HTTP://WWW.NEWYORKER.COM/REPORTING/ 2008/02/11/080211FA_FACT_STEWART?PRINTABLE=TRUE

Steve Schwarzman, who owns five trophy homes, is on the phone to somebody important. You can be sure he's not talking to the homeless person below.

A System Tilted Towards Those at the Top

Steve Schwarzman gives a blithe defense of his lavish excess. He says, " I just love homes." Does he even realize that he has so many homes he can't possibly live in all of them? Does he ever connect what he does in his job to the fact that over 2 million Americans lost their homes to banks last year? Does he realize that home mortgages in distress now exceed 4 million? Does he correlate this with the startling fact that the four million families are now in danger of losing their homes to big banks that received bailouts funded by taxpayers? Does he think that such an inequitable system is sustainable?

If you take away nothing else from this book, know that the whole game that governs our lives starts with a financial system skewed in favor of the big banks and those chosen few at the top of corporate America that the banks anoint with access to their credit. Know that we don't have to accept this system. We are all part of an ongoing personal and systemic evolution. There were many times I did not want to change my life, but crisis forced me to. *Abstracting from our own personal evolution, how can we not recognize what is happening in our midst? Our economic and environmental systems are burning up before our very eyes.*

In a varied career I've had an extraordinary opportunity to gain access to the top echelons of power and see the world at the top as few people see it. After a working for Chase Manhattan Bank a few years, I knew banking wasn't for me and I wanted to leave. Before I made a rash decision, a family friend, who had headed up the Chase REIT, suggested I talk with some of the other senior officers to get some "career advice." So he arranged a series of meetings, as sort of an extended counseling session. In those conversations, I got a glimpse of the lives those people lead and I knew it wasn't for me. I saw more the tired looks in their faces. I had seen their skewed values. I had seen the emptiness of their lives. I came away even more convinced that Wall Street banking was not for me. These executives, who all had "made it," also all seemed terribly unhappy. It was like they were lifeless and soulless. They were just going through the motions of extending credit and working out bad credits.

Advancing By Avarice

Many Wall Street bankers are thoroughly responsible and hard working people. Some even are enlightened souls who have a prophetic sense of where the world is headed. But even the best of them don't deserve financial rewards like this. Most are not rocket scientists. Usually the ones who rise to the top are not even nice people. They advance by avarice. Wall Street is polluted by pretenders–self proclaimed rulers of the universe, whose egos and temperaments are as volatile as the speculative swings of stock market that govern their lives. To become power brokers, they charge hard, trampling over

anything and anyone in their path. Most who rise to the top are arrogant SOBs who just know how to work the system. In their own self interest they abuse the system and corrupt it to their own advantage. We all pay the price for that. The tentacles of Wall Street grip all of us in an extended web of debt and deception. We all sense the whiff of corruption in their dealings. We all smell the stench coming from the government bailouts, but how exactly do these guys pull it off? We need to understand the precise nature of their power. How did they rise to such ascending heights.

My Moment of Epiphany

And yet, despite commanding the attention of the media we still have not yet hit upon the silver bullet that has can penetrate the amour of the system. Why? Because the inner working of the money and banking system are still a black box to most. What is lacking is understanding … understanding how banking really works.

Despite having worked inside the system for over two decades, I still didn't understand how the system **really** works until 2004, when I made my documentary film: *TIME BOMB: America's Debt Crises - Causes Consequences and Solutions.* That's when the lightbulb went on. During the making of that film, I had the proverbial "moment of epiphany" when I really came to understand how money is created and used to the advantage of established interests. One day during filming, I realized I was interviewing the people who were the system – renowned economists, powerful members of Congress and influential businesspeople.

Suddenly everything clicked. I could see the crisis that lay ahead and an even greater crisis looming – a crisis that would threaten the very foundations of American democracy. Since making the film, I have been increasingly concerned about both the stability and sustainability of our money and banking system, because the banking system is incorporates "moral hazard" that guarantees failure of institutions that are "too big to fail," and then transfer the costs bailing out those institutions to the taxpayers. Years before while at Chase Manhattan, I had pondered theses issues while sitting in classrooms of bank training classes, but it just didn't click. I learned how banks create money by simply making electronic notations on balances sheets. It wasn't until years later that I understood that this is all part of the design of the system. I suddenly grasped an unsettling truth about our money and banking system:

MONEY IS CREATED OUT OF THIN AIR BY BANKS WHEN THEY MAKE LOANS. MONEY IS THE MOST POWERFUL TOOL EVER CREATED, BUT IT HAS NO INTRINSIC VALUE. THE VALUE OF THAT MONEY IS ENTIRELY A FUNCTION OF TRUST IN THE BANKING SYSTEM. IF WE WANT TO TRANSFORM "THE SYSTEM," WE NEED TO THINK ANEW ABOUT THE WAY MONEY IS CREATED AND WHO CREATES IT.

Is Capitalism Just a Big Game?

Harvard Business School is sometimes described as the West Point of Capitalism. It's the place where the young capitalist cadets go to get scrubbed up and to learn the discipline of working in the system. I went there and endured two years in the pressure cooker. I'm glad I did. It taught me a lot about how the system works and the influences on the people who run the system.

On the occasion of my 25th reunion from Harvard Business School, received a fundraising letter from one of my old classmates, call him Joe, Bigshot, trying to convince me that Harvard Business School *actually needed more money*.

I found both the letter and its premise laughable. Of all the academic institutions in the world, Harvard Business School probably needs money the least. I called Joe and told him my reaction. He invited me into his office at the Transamerica Building, the big pyramid in downtown San Francisco to discuss it. He was an investment banker and the firm he worked for had just been acquired by Bank of America. In the transaction he cashed out his equity for over $20 million. A few years later he was named head of investment banking for Merrill Lynch. Joe and I chatted for awhile about the letter and other subjects. Suddenly the conversation turned philosophical. "John," he said,,

"IT'S ALL JUST A BIG GAME."

That was it. To guys like Joe Bigshot, it's all just a big game ... a game that leaves the the Wall Streeters at the top of the economic pyramid, like Joe, with more money than they know what to do with ... and others out on Main Street in a state of despair, destitution or desperation.

The last thing the world needs is another treatise on capitalism. We don't really pay attention to such things. But we do pay attention to the world of sports. We watch and listen intently as broadcasters and sports analysts fill our heads with useless information about batting averages, gains, strategies and scores - as if it really mattered. Meanwhile we pay no attention the play of the game that really affects our lives. What we need is something that takes apart the game of capitalism and brings its inner workings to light in a way that we can all understand. The big game of capitalism is composed of many individual players and plays. Let's start with the teams and the players on those teams.

The Teams and the Players

If Capitalism is just a big game, then who are the players and what are the rules? Who and what determines who wins? What are the teams and who are the players on the teams?

To oversimplify greatly there are two teams in the game of Capitalism: Wall Street and Main Street. Wall Street is a metaphor for the big players in the system. They're all part of a much larger ecosystem. Wall Streeters can be found not only in the world of finance, but also in the media, the law offices, the accounting firms, the consultancies, the universities, the halls of Congress and generally in plush offices

and tall skyscrapers of corporate America.

Main Street is a metaphor for the little guys who are getting left behind by the system. Main Streeters can be found in the factories, the cubicles, the hospitals, the churches, the firehouses, the classrooms, the stores and shops across America. An alarming number of Main Streeters aren't working at all these days. These are the players who are without the means to fight or system or change its rules.

The first and most fundamental truth about capitalism is that there are winners and losers. Because Wall Street has the power and understands the system better Main Street does, Wall Street always wins. In the last year, America has lost millions of jobs. This inequity between the big players and the little guys is endemic to the capitalistic system. Was this all part of the design of the system or just part of its evolution? It a bit of both. The game of capitalism is changing as we speak as its rules get refined. The mechanisms of excess and exploitation grow ever more sophisticated with each passing year. Where is this all leading us? We need to understand he hows and whys of capitalism, the rules and who the players are.

Wall Street - The Players

THE AGILE ACCOUNTANT: Nudges the numbers to make the balance sheets and P & L conform to CEO and investor wishes.

THE BLOATED BANKER: Rakes it in during good times and turns supplicant to government when the risky bets turn sour.

THE CORPORATE COOL: Serious swagger, debonair style and a heart of stone. Calls the plays that make or break the game.

THE CONNECTED CONSULTANT: Charges gazillions for designing the big plays, while abdicating any responsibility for their failure.

THE ECCENTRIC ECONOMIST: When Wall Street needs a big play, they turn here for bold new ideas, convoluted sentences, and supporting statistics to maintain the status quo.

THE FECKLESS FED: Charged with insuring the solvency and integrity of the financial system, their actions accomplish just the opposite.

THE INSECURE INVESTOR: Alway worried that they're going to lose their money, they still place big bets on risky businesses because they're connected to the market makers and addicted to gambling.

THE INSIDIOUS INSURER: Contracts are written to be nullified through nebulous language interpreted by the bureaucratic maze.

THE LUBRICATED LOBBYIST: Drinks, perks and campaign contribution keep the government well oiled with sufficient unction.

THE LOOPY LAWYER: Experts at finding loopholes in laws and contracts signed by well lubricated officials and operators of the system.

THE MINDLESS MEDIA: Their game plan is to distract and divert the electorate and populace from considering anything that really matters.

THE PLIANT POLITICIAN: Gets along by going along.

Main Street - The Players

THE ANGRY ACTIVIST: They say, "The system is broken. The System is unfair." and really wish they could get out of debt.

THE ARMY OF ARTISTS: Writers, musicians, filmmakers, bloggers, professors, clerics - architects all them ... soldiers in the trenches of this battle, using their creative expression as ammunition .

THE CUBICLE CRUNCHER: Staring at a computer screen all day, they try to appear busy so that their boss won't give them more work or a pink slip for slipping productivity.

THE DESPERATE DEBTOR: Behind on credit card or mortgage payments they pay usurious rates because they have no alternative.

THE DISTRACTED DOCTOR: Health care just isn't a high priority any more for a medical profession distracted by costs and craziness.

THE POPULIST POLITICIAN: Members of a colorful cast all fanning the flames of fear, anger and indignation while pandering for votes.

THE TERRIFIC TEACHER: You remember your favorite teacher. He or she works an entire lifetime to make what one of one Wall Streets titan makes in one whopping bonus just for speculating with your money.

THE ENRAGED ELECTORATE: Angry at the bonuses and bailouts, seeking ways to change the system that is screwing them royally.

THE INTERNET INSURGENT: These are the disruptors. They transformed the media and politics and might transform the banking sector. ...

THE SOCIAL SERVANT: Firemen, policemen, city clerks, librarians, and civil servants all striving just to keep pace economically.

THE WORRIED WORKER: Once proud, but in a global economy they're rendered impotent and obsolete by technology and outsourcing.

THE UNEMPLOYED UNCLE: Struggling in a world of economic hurt ... tries to make due on welfare and worry.

The Rules of the Game

All power players on Wall Street learn early that the rules of the game are written by cunning lawyers and legislators who know that all rules are created be bent to someone's advantage. So the key is to be that someone who will gain from the artful bending of regulations.

The name of the game is not to get caught. Wall Street has learned that there simply aren't enough referees who understand the game to possibly enforce all infractions. Rule bending is most profitable in periods of crisis, when new situations arise for which no rules have yet been written. Rule bending always involves a measure of risk, but the risks are controllable by devising a fallback strategy of plausible deniability. Almost all referee can either be bought at some price or

intimidated into submission. If you do get caught, deny, distract and mobilize influence on your behalf.

So then the ultimate object of the game is not only to acquire wealth but also to acquire influence. Money flows from power. Power flows from money. So the object of the game is to rise to the top in the game of money influence and power. This is accomplished through the right connections. Everyone is on the make for the right connections. Connection are acquired in many ways. Some come from old school ties. Some come through business associations. Some come from social events. Some come through charitable giving. Some come from serendipity.

True players in the power game realize that their most valuable asset is their time. So every moment must be spent with the right people cultivating relationships. Any time spend with someone without perceived power is time wasted. It's important never to return a phone call from someone who hasn't come with the right introduction.

On Wall Street public image is everything. Image comes from stature of the firm, the right manner of speaking, the right clothes, the right address, and of course, timing. Wall Street is winning the game of capitalism big time. But this won't necessarily always be the case. Main Street team has a potential star in the Enraged Electorate, but unless the Enraged Electorate is activated it remains an underperforming star.

Wall Street appears to have an insurmountable lead …. But wait … something is happening in the streets that changes everything.

Parody - U.S. Economy Grinds To Halt As Nation Realizes Money Just A Symbolic, Mutually Shared Illusion [2]

WASHINGTON—The U.S. economy ceased to function this week after unexpected existential remarks by Federal Reserve chairman Ben Bernanke shocked Americans into realizing that money is, in fact, just a meaningless and intangible social construct.

Calling it "basically no more than five rectangular strips of paper," Fed chairman Ben Bernanke illustrates how much "$200" is actually worth.

What began as a routine report before the Senate Finance Committee Tuesday ended with Bernanke passionately disavowing the entire concept of currency, and negating in an instant the very foundation of the world's largest economy.

"Though raising interest rates is unlikely at the moment, the Fed will of course act appropriately if we…if we…" said Bernanke, who then paused for a moment, looked down at his prepared statement, and shook his head in utter disbelief. "You know what? It doesn't matter. None of this—this so-called 'money'—really matters at all."

---

[2]. From America's Finest News Source, The Onion, FEBRUARY 16, 2010 | ISSUE 46•07; http://www.theonion.com/content/news/ u s economy grinds to halt as

"It's just an illusion," a wide-eyed Bernanke added as he removed bills from his wallet and slowly spread them out before him. "Just look at it: Meaningless pieces of paper with numbers printed on them. Worthless."

According to witnesses, Finance Committee members sat in thunderstruck silence for several moments until Sen. Orrin Hatch (R-UT) finally shouted out, "Oh my God, he's right. It's all a mirage. All of it—the money, our whole economy—it's all a lie!"

Screams then filled the Senate Chamber as lawmakers and members of the press ran for the exits, leaving in their wake aisles littered with the remains of torn currency.

U.S. markets closed as traders left their jobs and resolved for once to do or make something, anything of real value.

As news of the nation's collectively held delusion spread, the economy ground to a halt, with dumbfounded citizens everywhere walking out on their jobs ....

At the New York Stock Exchange, Wednesday morning's opening bell echoed across a silent floor as the few traders who arrived for work out of habit looked up blankly at the meaningless scrolling numbers on the flashing screens above. ... The realization that money is nothing more than an elaborate head game seems to have penetrated the entire country ... For some Americans, the fog of disbelief surrounding the nation's epiphany has begun to lift, with many building new lives free from the illusion of money.

The System is Broken

My awakening took the form of a questioning of the system itself. Bankers have a balancing act to play because money simultaneously serves public and private purposes. In was during this period that bankers and the banking profession in general started to change quite dramatically. Some of this change was spurred by legislation like the repeal of Glass Steagall which opened the floodgates to banks getting into investment banking and insurance. But more of the change had to do with bankers themselves becoming more greedy. Suddenly bankers started taking much greater risks with their capital, because the returns were there for the taking.

In the process capitalism itself started to develop its own form of an identity crisis. It was a profound shift we are just now beginning to understand its implications. Very few take issue with the capitalism in its ideal form, but the system has morphed into a dragon that few people want to defend. It has become a grotesque form of something that is grossly unfair while consuming scarce resources, financially and ecologically.

Today this identity crisis is playing itself out on the world stage. Our world finds itself on the brink of an unprecedented crisis of an epic proportions, from the sovereign debt crisis in Europe, to Congress' inability to tackle U. S. Debt issues, to student loan indebtedness to the mortgage mess. Many times in history the world has faced crises but never have they been of such magnitude and never before have so many of our most fundamental assumptions and institutions found themselves under such serious scrutiny. No institution is as fundamental to our crisis as the crisis of capitalism-the system we have chosen to organize our society. Whether capitalism is on the brink of catastrophic collapse, or simply putting forth a clarion call to change  depends upon our response. The root cause of our crises lies nowhere else but in our modes of thinking and the systems that support that thinking. We're in drift mode. We're headed together towards a reckoning .... the system upon which we all depend is broken ... What are we going to do about it? To them it's all a big game and they're winning ... Who will win this game? Wall Street or Main Street? You can be sure ... Wall Street is prepared to do battle.

***

Last fall, our financial system stood on the brink of a collapse that threatened a depression. The crisis required our government to display wisdom, courage and decisiveness. Fortunately, the Federal Reserve and key economic officials in both the Bush and Obama administrations responded more than ably to the need.

They made mistakes, of course. How could it have been otherwise when supposedly indestructible pillars of our economic structure were tumbling all around them? A meltdown, though, was avoided, with a gusher of federal money playing an essential role in the rescue.

The United States economy is now out of the emergency room and appears to be on a slow path to recovery. But enormous dosages of monetary medicine continue to be administered and, before long, we will need to deal with their side effects. For now, most of those effects are invisible and could indeed remain latent for a long time. Still, their threat may be as ominous as that posed by the financial crisis itself.

- Warren Buffett

NY Times, Op Ed, August 19, 2009, The Greenback Effect
http://www.nytimes.com/2009/08/19/opinion/19buffett.html

New Inequality Data and Polls Bolster Occupy Movement

A major study on income equality by a non-partisan government agency is likely to boost the "Occupy Wall Street" movement, whose standing with the general public appears on the rise, according to a new poll.

The study, released here Tuesday by the Congressional Budget Office (CBO), found that the average after-tax real income of the top one percent of the nation's households grew by 275 percent between 1979 and 2007 - about seven times greater than the increase in income by the remaining 99 percent over the same period.

And the income of the poorest 20 percent of the nation's earners grew by a mere 18 percent during that period, according to the report, which had been requested by the senior Democratic and Republican members on the Senator Finance Committee several years ago. That was less than one percent per year.

The report — the latest in a series of private or non-profit studies that confirm a sharp rise in income and wealth inequality over the past generation — came as a new New York Times/CBS News poll showed stronger-than-expected popular support for the "Occupy" movement, which has spread to dozens of cities across the country.

"The sense that most of us have been ignored by those in charge of economic policy is totally justified," said EPI economist and co-author of the report, Josh Bivens. "And I think it is what is driving the energy of the Occupy Wall Street campaign."

Jim Lobe - http://www.nationofchange.org/new-inequality-data-likely-boost-occupy-movement-1319728014

Troubling Questions Embedded in The System

There are troubling questions lurking deep within our system that few of us dare consider. Here are just a few of those questions:

- Is "The System" fair?
- If not … why not?
- What is the origin of power in our society?
- What is money?
- How is money created?
- What is the relationship between money and debt?
- Could money be created in a different way … by different people?
- What is the relationship between trust in government and our trust in money?
- Is our money system in its present form sustainable?
- Who and what determines how we value things in our society?
- How are our priorities established?
- Do those priorities reflect the true nature of the problems we face?
- What determines the value of money?
- What are the values embedded on our system?
- Who creates money and what are their motivations?
- What determines the value of money?
- What are the values embedded on our system?
- What is the true cost of all the money our government is borrowing?
- When will foreign investors start demanding higher risk premiums?
- At what point does the government reach its borrowing limit?
- Will the government's borrowing crowd out private credit needs?
- How will the government pay back all the money it's borrowing?
- Will the government have to monetize the debt?
- What are the risks of inflation and hyperinflation?
- Is the government's access to capital infinite?
- Is there a point when even our government doesn't can keep the system afloat?
- Is there a better way that doesn't involve so much risk?

UNLESS WE DEMONSTRATE A STRONG COMMITMENT TO FISCAL SUSTAINABILITY IN THE LONGER TERM, WE WILL HAVE NEITHER FINANCIAL STABILITY NOR HEALTHY ECONOMIC GROWTH.

- BEN BERNANKE. FEDERAL RESERVE CHAIRMAN

Gandhi's Wings: Occupy Wall Street and the Redistribution of Anxiety

We have reached a turning point. There is no more convincing people to play along in the "heads I win, tails you lose" game. We now plainly see that Atlas is strip mining our nation rather than carrying us on his shoulders of enterprise. The hero image of the business leader-provider is crumbling along with the core fabric of our society. Polls show that NYC citizens, Democrats and Republicans, and even Tea Party participants are all largely supportive of the protests. In Europe, many are ecstatic that America is finally objecting to the corruption at home that has been sliming the world for a long, long time. Etta James's "At Last" is being sung in the salons of Berlin and Paris.

Our secular religion of individualist economics is disintegrating in the face of a nightmarish experience. As the brilliant BBC Documentary film series by Adam Curtis entitled "The Trap: What Happened to Our Idea of Freedom" illuminates, the every-man-for-himself concept of society and freedom creates a horrible void. The Horatio Alger myth has been refuted and shattered by reality. That old myth was attractive emotionally -- promising to resolve anxiety by teaching that if you put your head down and worked hard you could control your own fate.

But that lie was exposed when Wall Street blew itself up and millions lost their jobs, their homes, and their pensions through no fault of their own. The reckless financiers took us all down with them, and there was no way to insulate ourselves from their casino games and their manipulation of government. And the games just go on. The menace of high frequency trading is only the latest example of a system rigged against us. But we have begun to question a perverted notion of freedom, where the only thing we protect is the rights of the powerful to plunder the commons. We see that this "freedom" is so destructive that it is threatening the very integrity of our much-hallowed capital markets. What an irony! Compulsive greed cannot resist consuming its own monuments.

by Robert Johnson, Director of Economic Policy, Roosevelt Institute, NewDeal2.0

Systemic Problems Need Systemic Solutions

Today, dire circumstances are pushing us into uncharted territory. Dire personal circumstances are pushing people into the streets to protest. Dire circumstances in the overall economy are pushing the Fed to assume unprecedented powers.

The severity or our recent financial crises made it clear that systemic problems now cry out for require systemic solutions. Our moment of reckoning has arrived and the birthing of Capitalism 3.0 is already upon us. There is a world of possibility awaiting us in the midst of our current economic crisis. The key to unlock this hidden potential is a new approach to *"The Money and Banking System."* The current system–*The 3C System*–concentrates economic power in the hands of private, profit making institutions whose primary fiduciary responsibility is to provide a financial return to shareholders. That fiduciary responsibility trumps any other consideration, including the interests and needs of the larger society.

The illusions surrounding our Money and Banking System ultimately doubles back upon themselves and stare themselves in the face, like an infinitely reflecting mirror of trust. Upon this trust has been constructed an entire edifice we call the global economy. It's an infinitely leveraged system built upon a foundation of debt that blows like sand in the wind. The debt based capital flows that are the lifeblood of our economy originate somehow, somewhere from within the inner sanctums of imposing temple-like structures in Washington, DC, huge banking towers that seem to touch the sky, and digital accounting entries that are as ephemeral as the 10 trillion dollars of wealth that simply evaporated during the recent liquidity crunch.

Today, there is righteous anger over the alleged fraud of bankers who were passing off toxic assets as sound investments; but this anger forgets about the long and distinguished tradition of swindling that has characterized the banking industry from its very inception. Student of economic history can cite a numerous examples of quick buck artists who chartered banks, issued bank notes and then absconded with the money, never redeeming the notes they issued. So the tradition continues with new tricks–financial innovations of increasing complexity invented at each new stage in the evolution of banking.

Fifteen years ago, the combined assets of our six biggest banks totaled 17 percent of our GDP. By 2006, that number was 55 percent. Right now, it stands at 63 percent.

- Simon Johnson
Author, 13 Bankers and
M.I.T. Professor

Almost $500 Billion Given to the 1% Every Year

On November 30, 2011, the morning after Standard and Poors, downgraded the credit rating of six major banks including Bank of America, Goldman Sachs, Citicorp, the major central banks poured more taxpayer money into the system, in effect, affirming one of the central messages of the Occupy Wall Street movement. What happened here is nothing more that the United States borrowing more money from China and others, to shore up the balance sheets of global banks, while U. S. taxpayers, pick up the tab, paying interest on the $15 trillion national debt. The interest on that national debt is now over $400 billion. This is all a huge transfer payment to the holders of those bonds … the 1% of the population that controls the wealth. But that's just one part of the systemic benefits that accrue to Wall Street.I

CENTRAL BANKS TAKE JOINT ACTION TO EASE DEBT CRISIS

WASHINGTON — PUBLISHED: NOVEMBER 30, 2011 - THE FEDERAL RESERVE MOVED WEDNESDAY WITH OTHER MAJOR CENTRAL BANKS TO BUTTRESS THE FINANCIAL SYSTEM BY INCREASING THE AVAILABILITY OF DOLLARS OUTSIDE THE UNITED STATES, REFLECTING GROWING CONCERN ABOUT THE FALLOUT OF THE EUROPEAN DEBT CRISIS. THE BANKS ANNOUNCED THAT THEY WOULD SLASH BY ROUGHLY HALF THE COST OF AN EXISTING PROGRAM UNDER WHICH BANKS IN FOREIGN COUNTRIES CAN BORROW DOLLARS FROM THEIR OWN CENTRAL BANKS, WHICH IN TURN GET THOSE DOLLARS FROM THE FED. THE BANKS ALSO SAID THAT LOANS WILL BE AVAILABLE UNTIL FEBRUARY 2013, EXTENDING A PREVIOUS ENDPOINT OF AUGUST 2012. "THE PURPOSE OF THESE ACTIONS IS TO EASE STRAINS IN FINANCIAL MARKETS AND THEREBY MITIGATE THE EFFECTS OF SUCH STRAINS ON THE SUPPLY OF CREDIT TO HOUSEHOLDS AND BUSINESSES AND SO HELP FOSTER ECONOMIC ACTIVITY," THE BANKS SAID IN A STATEMENT. ON WALL STREET, STOCKS RACED AHEAD AT THE 9:30 A.M. START OF TRADING IN NEW YORK, AN HOUR AND A HALF AFTER THE ANNOUNCEMENT BY THE CENTRAL BANKS. THE STANDARD & POOR'S 500-STOCK INDEX, A MEASURE OF THE BROAD MARKET, ROSE 3.2 PERCENT; EUROPEAN MARKETS WERE UP ALMOST 4 PERCENT IN LATE TRADING. THE PARTICIPANTS IN ADDITION TO THE FED WERE THE BANK OF ENGLAND, THE EUROPEAN CENTRAL BANK, THE BANK OF JAPAN, THE BANK OF CANADA AND THE SWISS NATIONAL BANK.
THE MOVE MADE CLEAR THAT REGULATORS INCREASINGLY ARE CONCERNED ABOUT THE STRAIN THAT THE EUROPEAN DEBT CRISIS IS PLACING ON FINANCIAL COMPANIES.

BY BINYAMIN APPELBAUM
THE WASHINGTON POST

I'm Changing My Name To Fannie Mae

By Tom Paxton

Everybody and his uncle is in debt,
And the bankers and the brokers are upset.
Goldman Sachs's, Merrill Lynch's
Saw themselves as lead-pipe cinches,

Now they've landed in the biggest screw-up yet.
Lehman Brothers and Bear Stearns and all their kind
Have turned out to be the blind leading the blind.
They are clearly the nit-wittest
In survival of the fittest—
Let me modestly say what I have in mind

Chorus:
I am changing my name to Fannie Mae;
I am changing it to AIG.
On this bail-out I am betting;
Just a piece of what they're getting,
Would be perfectly acceptable to me.

I am changing my name to Freddie Mac;
I am leaving for that great receiving line.
I'll be waiting when they hand out
Seven hundred million grand out—
That's when I'll get mine.

Since the first amphibian crawled out of the slime,
We've been struggling in an unrelenting climb.
We were hardly up and walking
Before money started talking
And it said that failure was the only crime.
If you really screwed things up,
then you were through;
Now—surprise!—there is a different point of view.
All that crazy rooty-tootin'
And that golden parachutin'
Means that someone's making millions—just not you!
(to chorus)

Part II

The Awakening
of a Banker

***

IT IS WELL THAT
THE PEOPLE OF THE NATION
DO NOT UNDERSTAND
OUR BANKING AND
MONETARY SYSTEM,
FOR IF THEY DID,
I BELIEVE,
THERE WOULD BE A
REVOLUTION
BEFORE MORNING.

- HENRY FORD

***

The Disconnect Between Wall Street and Main Street

I needed one more candid conversation before I stepped off the golden path. I needed to have a frank talk with my father about Wall Street. For forty years he worked for Bankers Trust Company at 16 Wall Street, joining the bank as a teller at the peak of the Great Depression in 1932 and, step by step, he rose to the top echelons of the bank, eventually becoming head of the Corporate Trust Department of what was then the seventh largest bank in the world.

I had only known the home life of my father, which seemed pleasant enough, never understanding what he really did for forty years commuting on the Long Island Railroad to those huge skyscrapers. We had a good talk. I asked my father how he had survived all those years in such a stifling environment. I'll never forget his response, "After a few years," he said, "you just get numb."

I didn't want that to happen to me, and took my father's startling admission as a ticket to escape Wall Street bondage for a freedom of sorts eventually working over a decade working on behalf of the homeless and the environment, I come away with a fundamentally different notion of what constitutes true success. Increasingly, I was drawn to the social and inner dimensions of success through social commitment. I could see clearly that most of what happens in the non profit world is ultimately constrained because they lack of access to the capital they need to scale good ideas. It all comes back to Wall Street and the fact that our existing money and banking system is completely disconnected from the real world concerns of Main Street. I was starting to awaken to the way banking is a two edged sword that cuts both ways in out society, building its financial clout upon illusions that escape public scrutiny.

10 Ways The Occupy Movement Changes Everything

1. It names the source of the crisis. The problems of the 99% are caused by Wall Street greed, corrupt banks, and a corporate take-over of the political system.

2. It provides a clear vision of the world we want. We can create a world that works for everyone, not just the wealthiest 1%.

3. It sets a new standard for public debate. Those advocating policies and proposals must now demonstrate that their ideas will benefit the 99%. Serving only the 1% is no longer sufficient.

4. It presents a new narrative. The solution is no longer to starve government, but to free society and government from corporate dominance.

5. It creates a big tent. We, the 99%, are made up of people of all ages, races, occupations, and political beliefs, and we are learning to work together with respect.

6. It offers everyone a chance to create change. No one is in charge. Anyone can get involved and make things happen.

7. It is a movement, not a list of demands. The call for transformative structural change, not temporary fixes and single-issue reforms, is the movement's sustaining power.

8. It combines the local and the global. People are setting their own local agendas, tactics, and aims. But we also share solidarity, communication, and vision at the global level.

9. It offers an ethic and practice of deep democracy and community. Patient decision-making translates into wisdom and common com-mitment when every voice is heard. Occupy sites are communities where anyone can discuss grievances, hopes, and dreams in an atmosphere of mutual support.

10. We have reclaimed our power. Instead of looking to politicians and leaders to bring about change, we can see now that the power rests with us. Instead of being victims of the forces upending our lives, we are claiming our sovereign right to remake the world.

- David Korten, Sarah Van Gelder and Steve Piersanti
Originally Published in Yes Magazine, Nov 10, 2011

A New Wave of Revolution

Today almost everybody knows about banks that are too big to fail. Those four words have become a rallying cry for the protests. The underlying unfairness and fallacy of those words has entered the mainstream of awareness, and have formed the basis of many of the Occupy Movement across the country. Simultaneous to these protests, young people are creating a new kind of revolution – a technological revolution. In many ways, they have been much more effective than the students of the late sixties in creating change, even though (or perhaps because) they are operating with the profit motive. I was privileged during the peak of the Internet boom, to be covering this revolution as a journalist with *Upside Magazine*. In that capacity I had a open access to the power elite in the high tech world, interviewing hundreds of entrepreneurs, CEOs and investors of companies that were changing landscape of business and society with new ideas and business models.

When I first contacted *Upside Magazine* in 1999, my first assignment was to cover an obscure search engine with a quirky name based in Mountainview, California. Back then few people beyond the Stanford campus or Silicon Valley tech circles had ever heard of Google. As a fledgling startup, Google's head of Google's Corporate Communications, was more than happy to block out a two hour slot on the schedule of Google's co-founders, Sergey Brin and Larry Page. I also spoke later with Google board members and VC funders, Michael Moritz and John Doerr as well as angel investors Andy Bechtolsheim, David Cheriton and Ram Shriram. Today, Brin and Page are billionaires and the investors in Google occupy five of the top six slots on the Forbes Midas List, which ranks the best dealmakers in high-tech.

I've often reflected on the serendipitous nature of that first *Upside Magazine* assignment. I had the opportunity to witness a revolution from the front row, by interviewing these guys at an early stage, to see at the source the nodes and networks that were springing from the ground up - all empowered by emerging technology - inspiring a new kind of the revolution that is changing the way the system works. ...

Yes, something profound is shifting ... suddenly the way we get our news is changing the the agenda itself .... When an injustice occurs suddenly the armies of the Web go into action ... witness what happened after a cop casually peppers sprayed peaceful protesters on the UC Davis campus ... the photoshop protesters went to work ...

THE HIGH GROUND THAT THE PROTESTERS SEIZED IS NOT AN ARCHIPELAGO OF PARKS IN AMERICA, BUT THE NATIONAL AGENDA. THE MOVEMENT HAS PLANTED ECONOMIC INEQUALITY ON THE NATION'S CONSCIOUSNESS, AND IT WILL BE DIFFICULT FOR ANY MAYOR OR POLICE FORCE TO

DISLODGE IT.

... THE STATISTIC THAT TAKES MY BREATH AWAY IS THIS: THE TOP 1 PERCENT OF AMERICANS POSSESS A GREATER NET WORTH THAN THE ENTIRE BOTTOM 90 PERCENT, ACCORDING TO AN ANALYSIS BY THE ECONOMIC POLICY INSTITUTE.

... THE SOLUTION TO THESE INEQUITIES AND INJUSTICES IS NOT SO MUCH SETTING UP TENTS AT BITS OF REAL ESTATE HERE OR THERE, BUT A RELENTLESS FOCUS ON THE COSTS OF INEQUALITY. SO AS WE MOVE INTO AN ELECTION YEAR, I'M HOPING THAT THE MOVEMENT WILL CONTINUE TO MORPH INTO: OCCUPY THE AGENDA.

- NICHOLAS D. KRISTOF

DOES THIS STORY SOUND FAMILIAR?

A GUY RIDES INTO TOWN ON A DONKEY. THEN HE SAYS THE
MONEYED INTERESTS ARE EXERTING TOO MUCH INFLUENCE ON
THE GOVERNMENT - AND ON SOME OF THE RELIGIOUS ELITE,
TOO. AND WHAT WAS THAT ABOUT THE WEALTHY? OH, YEAH -
"IT'S EASIER FOR A CAMEL TO PASS THROUGH A NEEDLE'S EYE
THAN FOR A RICH MAN TO ENTER HEAVEN."

3,000 YEARS OF MORAL LAW CONDEMNS PEOPLE WHO MAKE
EXCESS PROFITS FROM MONEY WITHOUT CONTRIBUTING TO
SOCIETY. EVERY SINGLE PROPHET TO MAKE THOSE ARGUMENTS
- WHICH IS TO SAY, ALL OF THEM - WAS CONDEMNED BY THE
PLUTOCRACY OF THE DAY. NO MATTER WHAT YOU BELIEVE OR
DON'T BELIEVE SPIRITUALLY, IT'S CLEAR THAT OLIGARCHIC
WEALTH HAS CORRUPTED OUR POLITICS, POLLUTED OUR
CULTURE, AND DEBASED OUR BASIC SENSE OF MORALITY.

EXCERPT FROM AND ARTICLE THAT WAS PUBLISHED AT
NATIONOFCHANGE AT:HTTP://WWW.NATIONOFCHANGE.ORG/
SEVEN-SNAPPY-COMEBACKS-THOSE-LAME-ANTI-OCCUPY-TALKING-
POINTS-1318344312.

The Fundamental Issues

Our money and banking System involves fundamental issues: How is money created? Who creates it and whose interest is served by the process of creating money? During pivotal periods of American history, the structure of *The Money and Banking System* was **the** burning issue in public debate. That debate focused on the role of big banks and the power they have to literally create money. To transform *The Money and Banking System* we need to ask, "Should banks and investment banks have the exclusive power to create money?"

FEW PEOPLE UNDERSTAND THAT THE POWER TO CREATE MONEY IS THE ESSENCE OF HOW "THE SYSTEM" REALLY WORKS. THE PURPOSE OF THIS BOOK IS TO ELUCIDATE THE ALCHEMY OF MONEY CREATION AND TO SUGGEST AN ALTERNATIVE THAT CAN AWAKEN OUR SLUMBERING ECONOMY, WHILE MOVING OUR SOCIETY TOWARDS THE ELUSIVE GOAL OF GENUINE ECONOMIC DEMOCRACY.

DO YOU KNOW HOW MONEY IS CREATED?

CENTRAL BANKING - AN UNHOLY ALLIANCE

IMAGINE BEING ABLE TO BORROW AND SPEND AS MUCH MONEY AS YOU WANT AND NEVER HAVING TO PAY ANY OF IT BACK. IMAGINE BEING ABLE TO WRITE AN IOU FOR EACH PURCHASE YOU MAKE AND HAVE SOMEONE ELSE REDEEM IT, OR BEING ABLE TO WRITE CHECKS AGAINST SOMEONE ELSE'S BANK ACCOUNT. IMAGINE HAVING THE LEGAL PRIVILEGE TO CREATE VIRTUALLY ALL OF THE NATION'S MONEY BY MAKING A FEW BOOKKEEPING ENTRIES AND LENDING IT OUT AT INTEREST. SHOCKING AS IT MAY SEEM, THIS IS THE NATURE OF THE MONETARY AND FINANCIAL REGIME THAT HAS SPREAD AROUND THE WORLD. BUT WHO HOLDS THESE PRIVILEGES AND HOW ARE THEY EXERCISED?

- THOMAS H. GRECO, JR
AUTHOR, THE END OF MONEY AND THE FUTURE OF CIVILIZATION

The Three "C" System

OUR EXISTING SYSTEM IS CONCENTRATED, CENTRALIZED AND COMMERCIALIZED. LET'S CALL THIS THE OLD SYSTEM OR THE 3C SYSTEM.

Unfortunately, *The 3C System* is dangerously flawed, because it relies upon an infinitely leveraged money created by big banks. *The 3C System* sacrifices the needs of Main Street to the greed of Wall Street. It's an answer that has left our society without sufficient capital to adequately address our most vexing social, environmental, educational, health care and political challenges. *The 3C System* values the private interests of a few over the public interest of many. The system rewards those who are creating phantom wealth, and punishes those who are doing hard and honest labor. *The 3C System* has forced the government to assume $12.8 trillion[3] in Federal commitments through bailouts and guarantees to prop up a flawed system. This is an astounding level of risk layered on top of an already fragile edifice of debt. *The 3C System* has resulted in fundamental imbalances, inequities and instabilities, that that today threaten the future of America. The 3C System system is infinitely leveraged and has become dangerously centralized and concentrated. It's due for an update, but first lets understand how money is created in the current system: *3C System.*

GIVE ME CONTROL OF A NATION'S MONEY AND I CARE NOT WHO MAKES THE LAWS.

- MAYER AMSCHEL ROTHSCHILD

---

3. Bloomberg Article - Mark Pittman and Bob Ivry, March 31, 2009 (Bloomberg)
http://www.bloomberg.com/apps/news?
pid=20601087&sid=armOzfkwtCA4&refer=home#

***

"ALL THE PERPLEXITIES, CONFUSIONS, AND DISTRESSES IN AMERICA ARISE, NOT FROM DEFECTS IN THEIR CONSTITUTION OR CONFEDERATION, NOT FROM A WANT OF HONOR OR VIRTUE, SO MUCH AS FROM DOWNRIGHT IGNORANCE OF THE NATURE OF COIN, CREDIT, AND CIRCULATION." - JOHN ADAMS, LETTER TO THOMAS JEFFERSON (1787-08-25), THE WORKS OF JOHN ADAMS

***

"THIS INSTITUTION (PRIVATELY-OWNED CENTRAL BANKS) IS ONE OF THE MOST DEADLY HOSTILITY AGAINST THE PRINCIPLES OF OUR CONSTITUTION...SUPPOSE A SERIES OF UNTOWARD EVENTS SHOULD OCCUR...AN INSTITUTION LIKE THIS...IN A CRITICAL MOMENT MIGHT UPSET (OVERTHROW) THE GOVERNMENT." - THOMAS JEFFERSON, DECEMBER 1803 LETTER TO TREASURY SECRETARY, ALBERT GALLATIN. HTTP://WWW.YAMAGUCHY.NETFIRMS.COM/7897401/JEFFERSON/GALLATIN.HTML

***

"I HAVE NO HESITATION TO SAY IF THEY CAN RE-CHARTER THE BANK (2ND BANK OF THE US - A PRIVATELY-OWNED CENTRAL BANK) WITH THIS HYDRA OF CORRUPTION THEY WILL RULE THE NATION AND ITS CHARTER WILL BE PERPETUAL AND ITS CORRUPTING INFLUENCE DESTROY THE LIBERTY OF OUR COUNTRY.
- PRESIDENT ANDREW JACKSON, APRIL 7, 1833 LETTER TO R. H. M. CRYER. RALPH CATTERALL, THE 2ND BANK OF THE U.S.

***

"WE SAY IN OUR PLATFORM THAT WE BELIEVE THAT THE RIGHT TO COIN AND ISSUE MONEY IS A FUNCTION OF GOVERNMENT. WE BELIEVE IT. WE BELIEVE THAT IT IS A PART OF SOVEREIGNTY, AND CAN NO MORE WITH SAFETY BE DELEGATED TO PRIVATE INDIVIDUALS THAN WE COULD AFFORD TO DELEGATE TO PRIVATE INDIVIDUALS THE POWER TO MAKE PENAL STATUTES OR LEVY TAXES...THOSE WHO ARE OPPOSED TO THIS PROPOSITION TELL US THAT THE ISSUE OF PAPER MONEY IS A FUNCTION OF THE BANK, AND THAT THE GOVERNMENT OUGHT TO GO OUT OF THE BANKING BUSINESS. I STAND WITH JEFFERSON RATHER THAN WITH THEM, AND TELL THEM, AS HE DID, THAT THE ISSUE OF MONEY IS A FUNCTION OF GOVERNMENT, AND THAT THE BANKS OUGHT TO GO OUT OF THE GOVERNING BUSINESS... WHEN WE HAVE RESTORED THE MONEY OF THE CONSTITUTION, ALL OTHER REFORM WILL BE POSSIBLE, BUT UNTIL THIS IS DONE THERE IS NO OTHER REFORM THAT CAN BE ACCOMPLISHED."
- WILLIAM JENNINGS BRYAN, CROSS OF GOLD SPEECH, 1896. HTTP://EN.WIKISOURCE.ORG/WIKI/CROSS_OF_GOLD_SPEECH .

How Money is Created in the 3C System

Most people believe that the government prints money on printing presses. This is a popular myth. The Fed regulates the amount of money in the M1 supply, but the Fed is not the government. It is a privately owned bank. The money that the Federal Reserve creates as coins, paper money and electronic notations represents less than ten percent of the $10 trillion dollars that slosh around our financial system. So how is the rest of our money created? Over ninety percent of the money that lubricates our economy is created by commercial banks. You make a deposit of $1000 at your local bank. If your bank is like most banks, it has a fractional reserve ratio of 10 to 1. This means that for each $1000 the bank holds on deposit, it can lend ten times that amount. So if the bank holds your entire $1000 on deposit, they can extend credit of $10,000. Where did the bank get the additional $9000? Did they have it in a vault someplace? No, the bank simply created it, with accounting entries. In the process, $9000 has been introduced to our financial system? Presto, $9000 is magically created by the bank, because this is what our fractional reserve banking system empowers them to do. The process doesn't stop there. That $10,000 in credit flows through the financial system and some of it gets deposited at other banks. Those banks then use those funds as deposits to make more loans. So it goes.

Investment banks also create money by creating stock in companies and they facilitating the sale of that stock in an Initial Public Offering. In either case, banks and investment banks are transforming worthless pieces of paper (or digits) into something that has market value simply by virtue of their stature as banks. Whey do we give banks a monopoly over this power? Could other social banks be created that distribute this power more widely in society?

"BANKS ACTUALLY CREATE MONEY WHEN THEY LEND IT. HERE'S HOW IT WORKS: MOST OF A BANK'S LOANS ARE MADE TO ITS OWN CUSTOMERS AND ARE DEPOSITED IN THEIR CHECKING ACCOUNTS. BECAUSE THE LOAN BECOMES A NEW DEPOSIT, JUST LIKE A PAYCHECK DOES, THE BANK . . . HOLDS A SMALL PERCENTAGE OF THAT NEW AMOUNT IN RESERVE AND AGAIN LENDS THE REMAINDER TO SOMEONE ELSE, REPEATING THE MONEY-CREATION PROCESS MANY TIMES."

- ON THE WEBSITE OF THE FEDERAL RESERVE BANK OF DALLAS
  HTTP://WWW.DALLASFED.ORG/EDUCATE/EVERYDAY/EV9.HTML

FROM ENRON TO OCCUPY AND BACK AGAIN
BY DAVID CALLAWAY, MARKETWATCH

THE ENRON MELTDOWN WAS 10 YEARS AGO THIS MONTH. ...

A DECADE ON IT'S CLEAR THAT THE ENRON COLLAPSE WAS JUST ANOTHER IN A LONG LIST OF SCANDALS THAT IN MY OWN CAREER BEGAN WITH DREXEL BURNHAM LAMBERT AND RAN RIGHT THROUGH MF GLOBAL A FEW WEEKS AGO. A GENERATION OF RISK-TAKING, OF GREED, OF LEVERAGE, OF EVER- MORE-DANGEROUS FINANCIAL INSTRUMENTS — FROM JUNK BONDS TO CREDIT DEFAULT SWAPS.

AT THE TIME OF ENRON'S COLLAPSE, EXECUTIVES WERE HEADING FOR TRIAL. POLITICIANS WERE DEBATING NEW REGULATIONS. AND AVERAGE INVESTORS WERE BLINDSIDED BY THE COMBINATION OF HUBRIS AND CORRUPTION THAT MADE NAMES LIKE KEN LAY, JEFF SKILLING AND ANDY FASTOW THE SYMBOLS OF CORPORATE GREED AND THE BUTT OF LATE-NIGHT TALK SHOW HOSTS.

NOW THOSE NAMES AND HEADLINES PALE IN LIGHT OF THE EVENTS THAT LED UP TO THE COLLAPSE OF BEAR STEARNS, OF LEHMAN BROTHERS, OF AMERICAN INTERNATIONAL GROUP, OF MF GLOBAL, AND OF THE NEXT BANK, POSSIBLY EUROPEAN, TO COLLAPSE.

THE EUROPEAN CRISIS, WHICH EXPLODED INTO THE NEWS WITH ICELAND'S PROBLEMS AND HAS STEADILY MARCHED EAST ACROSS THE CONTINENT, NOW THREATENS THE GREAT BANKS OF EUROPE, THE REGION'S SINGLE CURRENCY, AND THE HEALTH OF THE GLOBAL FINANCIAL SYSTEM. MARKETS TEETER AND LURCH FROM HEADLINE TO HEADLINE, THOUGH IT'S LIKELY THAT WHATEVER HAPPENS, WE'LL SURVIVE TO SEE THE DAY DOWN THE ROAD WHERE IT WILL BE SOMEONE'S COLLEGE THESIS.

ONE THING HAS CHANGED, HOWEVER. PEOPLE THIS TIME ARE ANGRIER. NOT JUST AT THE PARTICULAR COMPANIES LIKE AIG OR ENRON, BUT WITH THE ENTIRE CLASS OF HERMES-WEARING ARISTOCRATS WHO CONTINUE TO DEAL, TRADE, LEVERAGE AND SPEND AS IF THE OCCASIONAL BLOW-UP IS THE PRICE TO PAY TO DO BUSINESS.

ENRON WAS BIG BUT IT WASN'T GLOBAL. DREXEL WAS BIG, BUT IT DIDN'T THREATEN THE SYSTEM. EVEN THE COLLAPSE OF BARINGS PLS IN 1995 WITH THE ORIGINAL ROGUE TRADER, NICK LEESON, ONLY BRIEFLY THREATENED FINANCIAL INSTITUTIONS ACROSS EUROPE AND ASIA.

IT WASN'T UNTIL LEHMAN THAT THESE COLLAPSES REACHED A GLOBAL SCALE, AND PEOPLE REALIZED THE THREAT THESE BANKS CAN POSE TO THEIR OWN JOBS, LIVES AND FUTURES. NOW THAT WE'RE ON THE PRECIPICE AGAIN, THEY'RE ANGRY.

OF COURSE, THE LATEST CRISIS WILL PASS. ECONOMIES WILL RECOVER AND INVESTORS WILL MAKE MONEY AGAIN. BUT THE OCCUPY MOVEMENT, WHICH AT THIS MOMENT IS AT A CROSSROADS, HAS CHANNELED THE ANGER INTO SOMETHING THAT HAS SEIZED OUR CONSCIOUSNESS.

WE KNOW THEY ARE RIGHT. THE SYSTEM IS UNFAIR. WHAT CAN BE DONE?

A Oligarchy of Economic Power

The way money is created defines how economic power is distributed in society. The result? Wall Street bankers receive bailouts and fat green bonuses, Main Street workers receive default notices and thin pink slips.

Today, these privately owned commercial banks have an oligarchy over the power to create money through an ill understood financial alchemy known as the *fractional reserve banking system*. This system gives federally chartered banks an amazing power–the power to create money, by simply making accounting entries on their books. Banks don't have the money they lend to their borrowers. They create it out of thin air when they make loans, as long as they hold a small percentage of the loan on deposit with the Federal Reserve. Our most basic document, the U.S. Constitution, states in Article 1, Section 8, "Congress shall have the power to coin money, regulate the value thereof ..." but, our government has delegated that authority to private banks. THUS, WE HAVE PRIVATIZED PERHAPS THE MOST ESSENTIAL POWER OF GOVERNMENT: THE POWER TO CREATE AND CONTROL THE MONEY SUPPLY.

> I care not what puppet is placed on the throne of England to rule the Empire, ... The man that controls Britain's money supply controls the British Empire. And I control the money supply.
> - Baron Nathan Mayer Rothschild

WHAT IS BACKING UP THE $10 TRILLION DOLLARS IN MONEY THAT FLOWS THROUGHOUT THE FINANCIAL SYSTEM? NOTHING! NOTHING, BUT TRUST BASED UPON A SIGNATURE ON A LOAN AGREEMENT AND COLLATERAL OF UNCERTAIN VALUE, BACKS UP THE 10 TRILLION DOLLARS THAT ARE THE LIFEBLOOD OF OUR ECONOMY. *Few* of us consider the possibility that we can choose a new approach to creating *The Money and Banking System* and do it without congressional debate or legislative action. How? Very simply, by growing a decentralized and democratized money and banking system from the bottom up.

THIRTY YEARS OF UNLEASHED GREED

It is class warfare. But it was begun not by the tear-gassed, rain-soaked protesters asserting their constitutionally guaranteed right of peaceful assembly but rather the financial overlords who control all of the major levers of power in what passes for our democracy. It is they who subverted the American ideal of a nation of stakeholders in control of their economic and political destiny.

Between 1979 and 2007, as the Congressional Budget Office reported this week, the average real income of the top 1 percent grew by an astounding 275 percent. And that is after payment of the taxes that the superrich and their Republican apologists find so onerous.

Those three decades of rampant upper-crust greed unleashed by the Reagan Revolution of the 1980s will be well marked by future historians recording the death of the American dream. In that decisive historical period the middle class began to evaporate and the nation's income gap increased to alarming proportions. "As a result of that uneven growth," the CBO explained, "the distribution of after-tax household income in the United States was substantially more unequal in 2007 than in 1979: The share of income accruing to higher-income households increased, whereas the share accruing to other households declined. ... The share of after-tax household income for the 1 percent of the population with the highest income more than doubled. ..."

That was before the 2008 meltdown that ushered in the massive increase in unemployment and housing foreclosures that further eroded the standard of living of the vast majority of Americans while the superrich rewarded themselves with immense bonuses. To stress the role of the financial industry in this march to greater income inequality as the Occupy Wall Street movement has done is not a matter of ideology or rhetoric, but, as the CBO report details, a matter of discernible fact.

by Robert Sheer
HTTP://WWW.NATIONOFCHANGE.ORG/THIRTY-YEARS-UNLEASHED-GREED-1319808769

U.S. Near Bottom In New Social Justice Index

A central concern for those in the Occupy movement -- that the economic system in the U.S. is rigged in favor of the well-off -- has been corroborated by a major new survey of developed nations.

When it comes to social justice -- defined here as the ability each individual has to participate in the market society, regardless of their social status -- the United States ranks near the bottom of 31 developed countries, the Thursday report from the Paris-based Organization for Economic Co-Operation and Development (OECD) found.

It's one thing if you live in a market economy where everyone has the same shot at success. It's quite another if fortune favors the fortunate. And the OECD survey found that when it comes to "equal opportunities for self-realization," the U.S. ranks 27 out of 31 member states, well behind not just Northern European countries like Norway and Denmark, but even countries like Hungary, Poland, Italy and France. The only countries whose citizens fare even worse are Greece, Chile, Mexico and Turkey.

The new report comes just a day after theCongressional Budget Office validated another key precept of Occupy protesters: The income gap between the rich and poor in the U.S. grew precipitously from 1979 to 2007, the report found, with the top 1 percent of earners seeing their incomes spike by 275 percent.

The new OECD survey also echoes the findings of its own 2010 report on social mobility, which found that, contrary to America's reputation as the "land of opportunity," it is now much harder to climb the socioeconomic ladder between generations in the U.S. than in many other developed countries.

- Dan Froomkin, The Huffington Post - http://www.huffingtonpost.com/2011/10/27/social-justice_n_1035363.html

OECD Social Justice Index

1.	ICELAND	8.73
2.	NORWAY	8.31
3.	DENMARK	8.20
4.	SWEDEN	8.18
5.	FINLAND	8.06
6.	NETHERLANDS	7.72
7.	SWITZERLAND	7.44
8.	LUXEMBOURG	7.27
9.	CANADA	7.26
10.	FRANCE	7.25
11.	CZECH REPUBLIC	7.17
12.	NEW ZEALAND	7.14
13.	AUSTRIA	7.13
14.	GERMANY	7.03
15.	UNITED KINGDOM	6.79
16.	BELGIUM	6.73
	OECD AVERAGE	6.67
17.	HUNGARY	6.41
18.	IRELAND	6.41
19.	ITALY	6.29
20.	POLAND	6.17
21.	AUSTRALIA	6.14
22.	JAPAN	6.00
23.	PORTUGAL	5.97
24.	SLOVAKIA	5.96
25.	SOUTH KOREA	5.89
26.	SPAIN	5.83
27.	UNITED STATES	5.70
28.	GREECE	5.37
29.	CHILE	5.20
30.	MEXICO	4.75
31.	TURKEY	4.19

Source: OECD

HUFFPOST WORLD

The Battle Lines Are Drawn

If The Wall Street vs Main Street game escalates into full scale class warfare we risk the detonation of the debt Time Bomb. The result would be anarchy with social, economic, political and environmental dimensions. It won't be pretty folks.

The battle lines are being drawn. On the Main Street side, the power players are falling all over each other to be first in line to lead the "revolution." It's led to some bizarre combinations.

Liberal democrats like Bernie Sanders and Arianna Huffington are saying many of the same things as arch conservatives Sarah Palin, Rush Limbaugh, Ron Paul, Glen Beck, Shawn Hannity, and the Fox fair and balanced talk machine. All parties regardless of political persuasion are ratcheting up the rhetoric hoping for tectonic political shift. They railing against the bailouts, bonuses, banker and anything that smells of fat cats.

But these are mere skirmishes compared to what could be ahead. Today investing gurus are debating where we'll have a slow recovery or a bear market correction, but the can't see the forrest through the trees. The forest is a tsunami of political discontent that threatens to engulf our entire economic system. Folks, as we learned to our detriment in the subprime crisis, it only take a few people defaulting on their mortgages to bring down the entire system. Why? ... one word:

leverage.

A System Teetering on Collapse

Since our money is no longer backed by gold or silver, the entire financial system is infinitely leveraged. Today all money is created as debt. Greece, Spain, Ireland, Iceland and Portugal are but a mere ante in the high stakes poker game Wall Street likes to call "free market" capitalism. We've already seen two gargantuan bubbles form and burst in our midst: first the tech bubble, then the real estate bubble, but the ultimate bubble is forming in our midst: the bubble of governmental debt. If that bubble bursts, watch out!. It 's the meltdown where there is nobody left to

bailout the government. It's the meltdown where the curtain has been pulled behind the Federal Reserve's so called "ability" to stabilize the system. We're already seeing the vicious cycle of downward spiraling debt. There aren't enough fingers to go into the dyke. Are we feeling enough pain yet, to do something before the blowout that brings the entire system crashing down? What kind of system do we really want?

Dysfunction in government has brought the political process to a standstill. The Washington - Wall Street corridor has become a well trodden path with lobbyists inveighing themselves at every stage of budget allocation and legislative posturing. But without meaningful reform, the system itself is threatened. The wild swings in the stock market are telling us something. Where are the fundamentals of financial analysis? Our moment of truth is coming much faster than we realize. The time to act is now. The solutions are there if can start to see out the confines of conventional economic theory. If not, with the battle lines drawn, and government debt now at 14 trillion, there is insurance against what may become us. Without bold action, the system itself is headed for collapse.

The Dollar, The Euro and The Yuan

The United States retains its primacy in global financial markets for one primary reason: the Dollar is the default currency in the system. Why is this?

It's both simple and exceedingly complex. The United States is the world's dominant military superpower. We are also the world's dominant supplier of military

hardware. The House of Saud and other Middle East ruling families rely upon the United States for military support to preserve the legitimacy of their regimes. In return they provide the United States with the one thing that preserves Uncle Sam's primacy in the global financial system: petrodollars. The Mid East oil suppliers will only accept dollars for their oil. China, Europe and other oil consuming nations need oil. They can only pay for it in dollars. Thus they need dollars.

Get the picture. The United States dollar has value because of petrodollars. Now what happens if suddenly the allegiances shift. This is what is playing itself out behind the scenes in the global financial system right now.

So the world today is divided into two kinds of nations. Those that save and those that don't. The United States is a debtor nation … by far the world's largest. We owe more money than all the other nations in the world combined. China, Germany and others are saver nations. In other words, the number one export for the United States is the dollar. But this is changing … as China challenges the United States primacy in the global financial system.

China is engaged in a currency war with the United States. They don't want to take their marching orders from the United States any more. The United States is applying pressure on China through threatened boycotts like a cutoff of Iranian oil. China needs the oil. The United States need Chinese to keep buying our bonds. Nobody is happy. The system is unstable. When it unravels … as it must … Watch out. It's not going to be pretty.

PETRODOLLAR WARFARE

"THE FEDERAL RESERVE'S GREATEST NIGHTMARE IS THAT OPEC WILL SWITCH ITS INTERNATIONAL TRANSACTIONS FROM A DOLLAR STANDARD TO A EURO STANDARD. IRAQ ACTUALLY MADE THIS SWITCH IN NOV. 2000 (WHEN THE EURO WAS WORTH AROUND 82 CENTS), AND HAS ACTUALLY MADE OFF LIKE

A BANDIT CONSIDERING THE DOLLAR'S STEADY DEPRECIATION AGAINST THE EURO. ... "THE REAL REASON THE... CORPORATE-MILITARY-INDUSTRIAL NETWORK CONGLOMERATE WANTS A PUPPET GOVERNMENT IN IRAQ -- IS SO THAT IT WILL REVERT BACK TO A DOLLAR STANDARD AND STAY THAT WAY." (WHILE ALSO HOPING TO VETO ANY WIDER OPEC MOMENTUM TOWARDS THE EURO, ESPECIALLY FROM IRAN ... ALTHOUGH A COLLECTIVE SWITCH BY OPEC WOULD BE EXTREMELY UNLIKELY BARRING A MAJOR PANIC ON THE U.S. DOLLAR, IT WOULD APPEAR THAT A GRADUAL TRANSITION IS QUITE PLAUSIBLE. FURTHERMORE, DESPITE SAUDI ARABIA BEING OUR `CLIENT STATE,' THE SAUDI REGIME APPEARS INCREASINGLY WEAK/THREATENED FROM MASSIVE CIVIL UNREST. ... ALL OF THIS FITS INTO THE BROADER GREAT GAME THAT ENCOMPASSES RUSSIA, INDIA, CHINA.

- WILLIAM R. CLARK - AUTHOR: PETRODOLLAR WARFARE: OIL, IRAQ AND THE FUTURE OF THE DOLLAR

Debt The First 5000 years

by David Graber, Book Review

R. Caverly (Downingtown, Pa. United States)

Debt is a simple reality of everyday human interaction and at the same time a great moral calculus that rationalizes terrible suffering. It's power ranges from telling someone, "I owe you one", to the fateful words more and more Americans hear everyday: "The bank will be taking your house". Debt is both a thing that can be sold, traded, and securitized, as well as a space in which the most basic of human relationships begin.

David Graeber, an anthropologist ... but also an organizer in the Occupy Wall Street movement, has carefully and systematically sorted out the antinomies that surround the moral arithmetic of debt with the revealing bifocal lens of historical anthropology. His book is revolutionary in its answers to the what he says is the Great Question of debt ...

Graeber begins the book by challenging the founding myths of economics. Theories of capital always evolve out of the impossibility of a barter economy, but Graeber presents compelling evidence to the contrary, ... Debt is a relationship between two people who are "equals in those ways that are truly important", but are currently in a state of inequality, a state that must be resolved. Both parties seek to restore equality, but of interest are the things happen on that path to restoring equality. Debt as a temporary relationship of mutual need is far older than money, and has its own rules. His path to understanding the rules of debt, its importance in human relationships, and where debt goes wrong, is found in an examination of the the history of debt culture. ...

By the time Graeber reaches our modern world, he has begun to reveal that the "moral arithmetic" of debt can only be a product of violent enforcement of obligation; however, the contemporary system of obligation is entirely upside down. While we believe everyone has to pay their debts, this is demonstrably false, as the most powerful corporate entities in the world effectively had their debts paid for them in 2008. Coercion, the gun behind the loan documentation, reduces us to bare mathematics, often justifying what would otherwise be disgusting violations of life and liberty. ... I can't recommend this book enough.

MAJOR FOREIGN HOLDERS OF US TREASURY SECURITIES

Country	May 2009	Dec 2008	June 2008
SOURCE: US TREASURY			
China, Mainland	801.5	727.4	535.1
Japan	677.2	626	628
Carib Bnkng Ctrs	194.8	197.5	106.6
Oil Exporters	192.9	186.2	159.5
United Kingdom	163.8	130.9	55
Brazil	127.1	127	158
Russia	124.5	116.4	95.2
Luxembourg	96.3	97.4	102.6
Hong Kong	93.2	77.2	65.8
Taiwan	75.7	71.8	66.5
Switzerland	63.7	62.3	45.1
Germany	55.2	56.1	51.6
Ireland	50.6	54.3	19.9
Singapore	39.6	40.8	31.7
India	38.8	29.2	17.7
Korea	37.4	31.3	40.6

Mexico	31.6	34.8	41.1
Turkey	28.8	30.8	30.5
Norway	28.3	23.1	4.4
Thailand	26.8	32.4	31.2
France	25.9	16.8	15.4
Israel	19	18.8	9.8
Egypt	18.6	17.2	14.1
Italy	16.8	16	11.4
Netherlands	16.3	15.4	17.8
Belgium	15.7	15.9	15.4
Chile	14.7	15.2	12.2
Sweden	13	12.7	14.4
Malaysia	12.3	8.4	10.4
Colombia	11.9	11.1	9.2
Philippines	11.8	11.7	12.4
Canada	11.5	8.2	23.8
All Other	157.8	156.5	134.7
TOTAL	**3293.1**	**3076.9**	**2587.2**

What's wrong with this picture? America has become addicted to debt and can't kick the habit. America's business model is increasingly being exposed as smoke and mirrors. The whole model is unsustainable.

What Are the Stakes in This Game?

The stakes of this game cannot be overestimated. At stake is everything we hold dear to our way of of life, economically, politically and socially. If the American civil war almost tore the country asunder, so to this form of class warfare has the potential to bring our nation to its knees both domestically and internationally. Caught in the crossfire between the warring faction of the Wall Street PR machine and the Main Street political demagogues are the reasonable minds and voices. Their messages  are muted by a mainstream media that elevates the shrill above the sensible. The time has come for reasonable voices to speak up loudly. This is the purpose of this book: to encourage and embolden those who are genuine concerned about the extremes of thought that are now dominating the dialogue. Wall Street is not evil. They provide an essential service to our economy. But many of the practices of individual banks and bankers have put our entire system at risk. Their rewards are out of proportion to what they provide. The profligate risk takers must be recognized and dealt with firmly and fairly. But, the the political demagogues who seek to exploit this situation to their own advantage need to be countered by civility.

On both sides there is talk of conspiracies. Fingers point every which way, except to the root causes of our problems ... towards real solutions. But there is another conspiracy forming in our midst and this one is real. At our door are the wolves of China, India, oil producing and other asset rich nations who have ensnared our country in a growing web of debt, as effectively as Wall Street bankers have ensnared Main Street borrowers who succumbed to predatory lending practices. In the same way that wealth and has flowed to Wall Street financiers over the last century, power is now flowing towards those nations who have been more responsible in their use of money. How will we find our way out of this crisis?

OOPS ... IT'S ALL ABOUT TO
BOOMERANG

IN MICHAEL LEWIS' LATEST BOOK, "BOOMERANG," THE SUBTITLE
IS, "TRAVELS IN THE NEW THIRD WORLD." LEWIS IS NOT REFERRING
TO ASIAN OR LATIN AMERICAN COUNTRIES HERE. HE'S TALKING
ABOUT EUROPEAN COUNTRIES THAT DRANK THE ELIXIR OF
SEEMINGLY ENDLESS AND CHEAP CREDIT PRIOR TO THE BURSTING
OF THE RECENT FINANCIAL BUBBLE. TO SAY THAT CHEAP CREDIT
TRANSFORMED THE ECONOMIES IN GREECE, IRELAND AND
ICELAND, FOR EXAMPLE, IS TO UNDERSTATE THE IMPACT OF THE
FINANCIAL BUBBLE ON THESE COUNTRIES. TALK ABOUT A TIMELY
BOOK--I AM WRITING THIS DURING SEPTEMBER 2011, AND YET
THIS BOOK REFERS TO THE RECENT DOWNGRADE OF U.S. DEBT,
WHICH OCCURRED ONLY LAST MONTH, BEGINNING ON PAGE 171.

AS IN MANY OF LEWIS' BOOKS, THERE'S A NEW PERSON WHO YOU
PROBABLY NEVER HEARD OF BEFORE TO MEET. IN "MONEYBALL" IT
WAS BILLY BEANE, THE GENERAL MANAGER OF THE OAKLAND
ATHLETICS BASEBALL TEAM, AND IN "THE BIG SHORT" IT WAS
STEVE EISMAN, MICHAEL BURRY AND OTHERS. THIS TIME IT'S
KYLE BASS, THE MANAGER OF A DALLAS-BASED HEDGE FUND,
WHO LEWIS MAKES SOUND BOTH VERY INSIGHTFUL AND
ECCENTRIC. WHAT WOULD YOU CALL A MAN WHO OWNS A 40,000
SQUARE FOOT RANCH LOCATED ON THOUSANDS OF ACRES IN THE
MIDDLE OF NOWHERE WITH ITS OWN WATER SUPPLY AND AN
ARSENAL OF AUTOMATIC WEAPONS? OR SOMEONE WHO WOULD
RECOMMEND "GUNS AND GOLD" FOR HIS MOTHER? ANYWAY, THE
GIST OF BASS' FINANCIAL ANALYSIS IS THAT MOUNTAINS OF SHAKY
DEBT (ARISING FROM BORROWINGS DURING 2002 - 2006 BY
PEOPLE WHO COULDN'T REPAY) WAS ESSENTIALLY TRANSFERRED
FROM PRIVATE INSTITUTIONS (LIKE BANKS, ETC.) TO VARIOUS
GOVERNMENTS, TO THE POINT THAT EVENTUALLY MARKETS WOULD
QUESTION THE CREDIBILITY OF THESE GOVERNMENTS. PUT
DIFFERENTLY, THE PUBLIC DEBT OF CERTAIN COUNTRIES WASN'T
JUST THE OFFICIAL PUBLIC DEBT, BUT ALSO THAT WHICH CAME
FROM SUPPORTING VARIOUS PRIVATE INSTITUTIONS.

BASS, LEWIS TELLS US, VISITED HARVARD PROFESSOR KEN
ROGOFF (COAUTHOR OF "THIS TIME IS DIFFERENT: EIGHT
CENTURIES OF FINANCIAL FOLLY," WHICH I RECOMMEND), AND
FOUND EVEN ROGOFF TO BE SURPRISED BY THE MAGNITUDE OF
THE PUBLIC DEBT PROBLEMS.

- FROM ADAMSMYTHE'S AMAZON REVIEW OF BOOMERANG BY
MICHAEL LEWIS

Is the Big One Coming?

If the "Big One" is really coming soon, it will be bigger than the 2000 dot-com crash and the 2008 subprime credit meltdown combined. A huge market blowout. Bloomberg-BusinessWeek writes: "The results won't be pretty for investors or elected officials." If the global-debt bomb explodes don't expect a typical bear correction followed by a new bull. Wall Street's toxic pseudo-capitalism is imploding. Be prepared for a massive meltdown. Yes, already the third major bubble-bust of the 21st century, triggered once again by Wall Street's out-of-control Fat Cat Bankers. And it's dead ahead.

Can your family survive in the anarchy after the debt bomb explodes? America's already at a historic a turning point that must bleed through a no-man's land of lawless self-destructive anarchy before a neo-capitalistic world can re-emerge. Investors tell me they "feel" it at a deep level, "know" it's happening. They keep asking: "What's the best investment strategy to prepare now?"

This is no joke, folks. Are you prepared? Or preparing? Will your family survive in a post-apocalyptic world, when anarchy is rampant in America? Look at Washington, Wall Street and Corporate America today. You know it's already begun.

You are witnessing a fundamental breakdown of the American dream, a systemic breakdown of our democracy and our capitalism, a breakdown driven by the blind insatiable greed of Wall Street: Dysfunctional government, insane markets, economy on the brink. Multiply that many times over and see a world in total disarray. Ignore it now, tomorrow will be too late.

This is Not a war about ideology, but about finding an economic game-changer. For Wall Street the question asked is: "If the big one is coming, how do I invest? Do I invest in gold? But buying Gold has already reached bubble like proportions. What about commodities? Can I hedge my bets by going short?

Main Street asks, "Should I hoard cash? What happens if the bear market continues on for years or decades? "What about those who have no cash? What about their families? What can I do if I get laid off or if I can't find a job?

Monetary Madness

Money is the most powerful tool ever created by humans. The value of our money is entirely a function of trust. This faith in our money is the basis of all commercial interaction.

In our current money and banking system there is a disconnect between the process of wealth creation and the process of value creation. There is a disconnect between value and values. There is a disconnect between money and meaning in our lives. It doesn't have to be like this. There is a better way to integrate money with

meaning, value with values.

For almost a hundred years we have been working with the same monetary and banking system, despite a radically altered landscape of business and society. The time has come to move beyond the rhetoric about new regulation. The time has come to towards sustainable solution to our money and banking crisis that can harness the inherent good within each of us and channel it towards the common good. Our current crisis forces us to think anew.

The process by which money is created today is ill understood by the general populace. Most people think that governments create money either on printing presses or electronically. This is only partially true. Government created currency represents less than ten percent of all the money in circulation. So where does the rest of our money come from? It is created by commercial banks through a financial alchemy called the fractional reserve banking system. Whenever banks extend credit, they are in effect creating money. The amount of credit banks can extend is regulated by central banks. Reserve requirements are generally one dollar of reserves for each ten dollars of bank credit extended.

Since money is created in this process of extending credit, our entire economy is essentially build upon a foundation of promises to repay. Thus, our financial system is infinitely leveraged because there is nothing backing up bank created money, other than a signature on a piece of paper or collateral of uncertain value. As such the value of money and stability of our economy is entirely a function of trust. Trust is the glue of the system. If trust erodes, the system breaks down. We have witnessed this simple fact in the current credit crisis. This is the nature of an interest based monetary / banking system. The essential point is this: over ninety percent of official currency in circulation today is created by commercial banks as debt  whenever they extend credit to a borrower. The rest is created through accounting entries in an exchange between the U. S. Treasury and The Federal Reserve.

But not all monetary systems are interest based, and not all monetary systems reward private interests quite as powerfully as our present monetary system. If the power to create money were invested not only with private banks, but also with businesses and groups in society that are motivated by some overriding public or social purpose, it would revitalize all manner of organizations and people who are motivated to somehow make the world a better place or improve their lives. It would also act as a flywheel, stabilizing the existing banking system, because those most likely to default would have a safety net.

As America descends into economic malaise, the average income on Main Street is $50,000, but this is a mere pittance compared to the average bonuses paid to Wall Street's bankers. What if you're one of the 10 % or the of 20% underemployed. Will Food Stamps see your through? What if you suffer a medical emergency and you're one of the almost 50 million with no medical insurance?

These are the questions asked on opposite sides of class warfare. Is there is an alternative? Is a Second American Revolution coming out of the nascent movements. Will it take great crisis to awakens America? Will it take a systemic shock before we look into the system that got us in this predicament?

Why Obama Won't Be Able To Reform Wall Street

Listening to President Obama's heartfelt, well-intentioned, but ultimately naïve speech on financial reform today, my mind kept flashing on a story I heard the last time Washington, in the wake of the Enron scandal, promised to reform Wall Street. The story came from a friend who took a family trip on a cruise ship. Her 10-year-old son kept pestering the crew, begging for a chance to drive the massive ocean liner. The captain finally invited the family up to the bridge, whereupon the boy grabbed hold of the wheel and began vigorously turning it. My friend panicked -- until the captain leaned over and told her not to worry, that the ship was on autopilot, and that her son's maneuvers would have no effect. And that's the way it is with our leaders. They stand on the bridge making theatrical gestures they claim will steer us in a new direction while, down in the control room, the autopilot, programmed by politicians in the pocket of special interests, continues to guide the ship of state along its predetermined course. Standing on the deck at historic Federal Hall, the president said all the right things, eloquently pointing out how American taxpayers had "shouldered the burden of the bailout" and are "still bearing the burden of the fallout -- in lost jobs, lost homes, and lost opportunities." And I don't dispute for a minute that his heart is in the right place, and that he means it when he says "the old ways that led to this crisis cannot stand" and touts "the need for change and change now." But we've been hearing similarly great sentiments for months now -- and they've had the same impact as my friend's ten year-old yanking on the cruise ship wheel. None. President Obama won't be able to change the course our financial system is on unless he goes down into the boiler room and disengages the autopilot -- which means taking on the bankers and their hordes of lobbyists who continue to dictate policy in DC. To do that, the president will have to do more than deliver great speeches. He'll need to stand firm when the lobbyists, working behind the scenes, work to gut real reform, leaving only the appearance of reform in its place. This is exactly what he failed to do when the banking lobbying killed cramdown legislation back in April. But instead of telling the Wall Street power players watching him today that he was going to insist on making cramdown a part of his financial reform package, he tried to appeal to their better angels, reminding them that they didn't have to wait for Congress to pass new laws... they could just start acting better on their own. It was shockingly naïve. Wall Street has been spending hundreds of millions of dollars, doing everything in its power to kill things like cramdown legislation, derivatives regulation, and the proposed Consumer Financial Protection Agency, and the president is asking them to be nicer people. That's like tossing a wounded seal into the middle of a school of Great White sharks and hoping the beasts will nurse it back to health.

Arianna Huffington, The Huffington Post, Sept 14, 2009

Is Our Money System a Ponzi Scheme?

It seemed to be the best of times. Then suddenly things changed. Bankers stopped trusting each other. Capital markets seized up and the flow of credit came to a screeching halt. The situation was unraveling quickly. Unless Congress acted, they were told there was the risk of a complete breakdown of the U.S. financial system. The potential consequences of inaction were too dire to consider, so Congress acted quickly. A $789 billion dollar bailout was approved as a down payment on over $12 trillion of government bailouts, subsidies and guarantees. W e will never know what might have happened if Congress had not acted; but the warnings were real.

With a financial system that is infinitely leveraged, over $50 trillion dollars of wealth, is backed up by nothing other than trust in the system. In a matter of months, over $10 trillion of that wealth simply evaporated as trust in the system dissipated. It could have been much worse. It still might be....

Whether our banking system is a giant Ponzi scheme is an open question. Nobody in a position of power will ever openly discuss this contention, because honest discussion about the sustainability of the system will guarantee failure of the system. Even mild doubts about long term viability of the banking system expressed publicly by people in high places would send shock waves through financial markets. Doubt would spread like a contagion and dissipation of trust would become a self-fulfilling prophesy.

Increasingly it has become apparent Wall Street has become dangerously centralized, concentrated and commercialized. In the late 1970s, Wall Street's share of corporate profits in America was somewhere around 17%. Since then Wall Street's slice of the pie, has more than doubled to over 40%. During this period the character of Wall Street bankers has changed in fundamental ways and their appetite for risk has increased dramatically.

THE MADNESS OF MADOFF

"IN 2006, THE SEC DISCOVERED MR. MADOFF MISLED THE AGENCY ABOUT THE NUMBER OF INVESTORS HE WAS MANAGING AND THE NATURE OF THE STRATEGY HE USED, AMONG OTHER PROBLEMS, ... THE AGENCY REQUIRED MR. MADOFF TO REGISTER HIS FIRM AS AN INVESTMENT-ADVISORY BUSINESS BUT DIDN'T PURSUE THE CASE FURTHER. ... REPRESENTATIVES OF THE SEC ... DEFENDED MISSING THE FRAUD THAT IS BELIEVED TO HAVE SPANNED MORE THAN THREE DECADES. FINRA'S STEPHEN LUPARELLO SAID THE BROKERAGE INDUSTRY'S SELF-REGULATORY BODY WASN'T AWARE THAT THE MADOFF FIRM WAS MANAGING MONEY FOR INVESTORS. ... WE WERE NEVER RECIPIENTS OF RED FLAGS THAT LED US TO HAVE SKEPTICISM ABOUT THAT," HE SAID. ... SEN. BOB CORKER (R., TENN.) RESPONDED, "THAT SEEMS HARD TO DIGEST." SEN. CHRISTOPHER DODD (D., CONN.), CHAIRMAN OF THE COMMITTEE, CALLED THE ALLEGED MADOFF FRAUD "A REGULATORY FAILURE OF HISTORIC PROPORTIONS." ... SEC OFFICIALS SAID THEY WERE UNDERSTAFFED TO DEAL WITH THE FAST-GROWING INVESTMENT-ADVISORY BUSINESS AND TRIED TO CONDUCT EXAMINATIONS AS FREQUENTLY AS THEY CAN. ... SEVERAL SENATORS QUESTIONED THE QUALITY OF THE SEC'S EXAMS AND ITS HANDLING OF COMPLAINTS, ESPECIALLY THE 20-PLUS PAGE REPORT FROM HARRY MARKOPOLOS, A FORMER INDUSTRY EXECUTIVE, WHO IN 2005 SUGGESTED THE MADOFF FIRM WAS A GIANT PONZI SCHEME. "THOSE OF US IN THE ENFORCEMENT DIVISION WANT TO BRING CASES. WE WANT TO GET EVERY PONZI SCHEMER, EVERY MARKET MANIPULATOR," MS. THOMSEN SAID. "IT IS A SAD TRUTH THAT SOMETIMES THEY GET AWAY WITH THINGS FOR SOME PERIOD OF TIME. I HATE THAT."

Ponzi Schemes are always looking for another sucker. Bernie Madoff knew this well. But, Madoff, was but a symptom of the disease. Ponzi schemes, by definition, must eventually fail. The "powers that be" at the Fed and Treasury, however, have made it clear that they won't let our banking system collapse. They will pump enough money into the system to keep it going. When the Fed needs money it creates it out of thin air through electronic entries. All of this is hidden from public view with good reason.

Intelligent people of diverse of economic viewpoints predicted this crisis. They include: Nouriel Roubini, David Walker, Nassim Nicholas Taleb, Joseph Stiglitz, Stephen Roach, Stephanie Pomboy, Naomi Klein, William Greider, Robert D. Manning, Danny Schechter, Juliet Schor, Alf Field, Marc Faber, Richard Rainwater, George Soros, Peter Schiff, Bob Bixby, Martin Weiss, Robert Prechter, David Tice, James D. Scurlock, Elizabeth Warren and Paul Krugman. The inner workings of the system are flawed. Is that flaw fundamental to the system's survival? That's the question we must answer before it's too late.

Money Myths

Most people believe that the government prints money on printing presses. This is a popular myth. The Fed regulates the amount of money in the M1 supply, but the Fed is not the government. It is a privately owned bank. The money that the Federal Reserve creates as coins, paper money and electronic notations represents less than ten percent of the $10 trillion dollars that slosh around our financial system. So how is the rest of our money created? Over ninety percent of the money that lubricates our economy is created by commercial banks.

Today, these privately owned banks have a virtual monopoly over the power to create money through an ill understood financial alchemy known as the *fractional reserve banking system.* This system gives federally chartered banks an amazing power–the power to create money, by simply making accounting entries on their books. Banks don't have the money they lend to their borrowers. They create it out of thin air when they make loans, as long as they hold a small percentage of the loan on deposit with the Federal Reserve. Our most basic document, the U.S. Constitution, states in Article 1, Section 8, "Congress shall have the power to coin money, regulate the value thereof ..." but, our government has delegated that authority to private banks. *Thus, we have privatized perhaps the most essential power of government: the power to create and control the money supply.*

> I CARE NOT WHAT PUPPET IS PLACED ON THE THRONE OF ENGLAND TO RULE THE EMPIRE, ... THE MAN THAT CONTROLS BRITAIN'S MONEY SUPPLY CONTROLS THE BRITISH EMPIRE. AND I CONTROL THE MONEY SUPPLY.
>
> - BARON NATHAN MAYER ROTHSCHILD

The Paradox of Our Government Paper

Our current money system is governed by a paradox–a paradox so powerful in its simplicity that few of us ever give it a thought. The paradox is this:

OUR MONEY HAS NO INTRINSIC VALUE. THE VALUE OF OUR MONEY IS ENTIRELY A FUNCTION OF THE TRUST WE PLACE IN THE SYSTEM THAT SUPPORTS IT. IF THIS TRUST DISSIPATES TO A POINT OF RECKONING, A COLLAPSE IN THE SYSTEM THAT SUPPORTS OUR MONEY IS INEVITABLE.

THERE IS NOTHING BUT TRUST IN THE SYSTEM BACKING UP THE $10 TRILLION IN CURRENCY THAT CIRCULATES AS THE LIFEBLOOD OF OUR ECONOMY.

Consider this startling fact: *before the current crop of fiat based currencies, virtually every fiat based currency in history has eventually collapsed.* From the debasement of the Denarius and the fall of the Roman empire ... to the civil unrest created in part by a rapidly expanding currency under Marco Polo ... to John Law's failed experiments with paper money in France ... to the assignats in France that were inflating at approximately 13,000% ... to Weimar Germany, when inflation got so bad that German citizens were using wheelbarrows of money to buy a loaf of bread ... to 1932, when Argentina's currency collapsed ... to 1992, when Finland, Italy, and Norway sent currency shocks waves of panic throughout Europe ... to 1994, when Mexico and the infamous "Tequila Hangover" spread economic hardships throughout Latin America ... to 1997, when the effects of the plummeting Thai baht spread to Malaysia, the Philippines, Indonesia, Hong Kong, and South Korea... to 1998, when the devaluation of the Russian ruble wrought the breakup former Soviet Union ... to 2008, with the collapse of the Icelandic economy. No fiat currency before our current crop has survived indefinitely. Even American has not been immune. Two U.S. government backed currencies have already failed. The "Continental" failed in the revolutionary war and the "Greenback" failed after the Civil War. Life After the Meltdown - When the markets crashed, a whole intellectual edifice fell with them. New economic ideas are needed.

A Global Gambling Casino

During the buildup of the bubble, it was "don't ask, don't tell" for the financial industry. These risky loans were then lumped together, packaged as CDOs and sold on a secondary market. It was a disaster in the making, made all the worse by the sense of inebriation in the marketplace, and the bonuses that were being awarded to those who were complicit in the system.

The FBI regulators who normally might have been on the watch, were pulled off the case and transferred to what was deemed a higher national priority at

the time – hunting down potential terrorists in the wake of 9/11. The rating agencies became complicit in the charade by proffering "no risk," Triple A ratings to securities that were clearly high risk. This was, and still is, a formula for a highly unstable - and inequitable - system.

IT'S A SYSTEM CHARACTERIZED BY SPECULATIVE STOCK MARKET SWINGS - AND SWINDLES. BEWARE OF THE BULL. STOCK MARKET HAS BECOME GLOBALIZED GAMBLING CASINO AND WALL STREET OWNS THE CASINO.

Wall Street analysts pump up stock prices of banks, while workers on Main Street work harder and get paid less. Main Street workers run faster and faster on a treadmill of debt, but fall farther and farther behind in credit card and mortgage payments to the big banks.

This is a fundamental flaw of our current money system.

FINANCIAL LITERACY IS A BIG FAT WALL STREET HOAX

Financial-literacy programs are getting popular again. Warning: They don't work. Maybe for 7% of us. But for the rest of Americans, they are a big waste of your time, and your money. Financial-literacy programs reveal a subtle lesson in behavioral economics brainwashing. Why? Your brain is irrational, you can't rewire or reprogram it. But Wall Street can. They have seven clever ways to turn your irrational behavior against you, to manipulate you, to siphon off your money.

Financial Literacy will never work. Never. Want proof? Just think about the past decade: Factor in the 2000 dot-com crash, the 30-month recession, the 2008 meltdown and guess what: On an inflation-adjusted basis Wall Street lost 20% of America's retirement money in the 2000-2010 decade. And they'll do it again. Get it? Financial literacy is a cruel joke Wall Street insiders keep playing on investors, local governments, school systems, Congress and the President. Here's the problem why even the best-of-intention programs will never (yes, never) work: They assume, erroneously, the human brain can retrain itself to make rational decisions about investing, finance and budgeting. But that's impossible.

Your brain is your worst enemy, always irrational, easily manipulated When it comes to investing, no matter how intellectually gifted you are, emotions will trump reason. Solution: Daniel Kahneman, Princeton psychology professor and Nobel economist says we "would be better investors if we just made fewer decisions." But we don't. Even professionals, the "people who are specifically trained to bring" rational decision-making skills "to problems, don't do so even when they know they should."
You simply cannot rewire and reprogram an irrational brain and make an investor "less irrational." And yet, as well-intentioned as they are, the financial-literacy idealists keep fighting a losing battle, they're like Don Quixote tilting at wind mills.

By PAUL B. FARRELL, MarketWatch

Depositors line up outside a branch of Washington Mutual Bank on Sep 26, 2008. With $307 billion in assets, WaMu was by far the biggest bank failure in history, eclipsing the 1984 failure of Continental Illinois.

THE AVERAGE AMOUNT OF TIME A STOCK IS HELD ON THE NEW YORK STOCK EXCHANGE ... 3 SECONDS. THIS IS WHAT THE SYSTEM IS ALL ABOUT ... TRADING AT THE SPEED OF LIGHT TO TAKE ADVANTAGE OF THE SMALL INVESTOR WHO HAS NO CLUE WHAT IS REALLY GOING ON BEHIND THE SCENES ON THE TRADING FLOOR.

Debt Slavery

Crushing debt has created a modern and insidious form of slavery for millions who fear default. Our current debt based currency system is essentially a mechanism for creating *debt slavery*. People are debt slaves to big banks whose only right to the money they are creating is their charter with the government.

> ## "DEBT IS THE SLAVERY OF THE FREE."
> - PUBLILIUS SYRUS (ROMAN AUTHOR, FIRST CENTURY B.C.)

Guess what? This is the way the system is designed.

This situation concentrates power in the hands of profit making institutions whose primary fiduciary responsibility is to provide a return to shareholders - to the exclusion of the interests and needs of the larger society. Some people have described our banking system as a giant Ponzi scheme. Ponzi schemes, by definition, must eventually fail. The "powers that be" at the Fed and Treasury, however, have made it clear that they won't let our banking system collapse. They will pump enough money into the system to keep it going.

This situation concentrates power in the hands of profit making institutions whose primary fiduciary responsibility is to provide a return to shareholders - to the exclusion of the interests and needs of the larger society. Some people have described our banking system as a giant Ponzi scheme. Ponzi schemes, by definition, must eventually fail. The "powers that be" at the Fed and Treasury, however, have made it clear that they won't let our banking system collapse. They will pump enough money into the system to keep it going.

The Core of The System: The Fed

Populist preoccupation with issues surrounding out money and banking system subsided, until a solution was put forth with a sense of finality – a solution created in the secrecy of a gathering of elite bankers on Jekyll Island. Thus, in 1913, *The Money Question* was seemingly "resolved" when President Woodrow Wilson signed into law the Federal Reserve Act empowering centralized banks to create money through a fractional reserve banking system. Later President Wilson regretted having signed that act. He rued,

"I HAVE UNWITTINGLY RUINED MY COUNTRY."

THE BIRTH OF THE FEDERAL RESERVE SYSTEM

THE PURPOSE OF THE MEETING ON JEKYLL ISLAND WAS NOT TO HUNT DUCKS. SIMPLY STATED, IT WAS TO COME TO AN AGREEMENT ON THE STRUCTURE AND OPERATION OF A BANKING CARTEL. THE GOAL OF THE CARTEL, AS IS TRUE WITH ALL OF THEM, WAS TO MAXIMIZE PROFITS BY MINIMIZING COMPETITION BETWEEN MEMBERS, TO MAKE IT DIFFICULT FOR NEW COMPETITORS TO ENTER THE FIELD, AND TO UTILIZE THE POLICE POWER OF THE GOVERNMENT TO ENFORCE THE CARTEL AGREEMENT. IN MORE SPECIFIC TERMS THE PURPOSE AND, INDEED, THE ACTUAL OUTCOME OF THIS MEETING WAS TO CREATE THE BLUEPRINT FOR THE FEDERAL RESERVE SYSTEM. ... THE PRIMARY OBJECTIVE OF THIS CARTEL IS TO INVOLVE THE FEDERAL GOVERNMENT AS AN AGENT FOR SHIFTING THE INEVITABLE LOSSES FROM THE OWNERS THESE BANKS TO THE TAXPAYERS.

- G. EDWARD GRIFFIN
AUTHOR, THE CREATURE FROM JEKYLL ISLAND

The Birth of the System

In the secrecy of a gathering of elite bankers on Jekyll Island the blueprint for the Federal Reserve System was born in 1913. Later that year, President Woodrow Wilson signed into law the Federal Reserve Act empowering centralized banks to create money through a fractional reserve banking system. Later President Wilson regretted having signed that act. He rued, "I have unwittingly ruined my country."

In comparison to the snake oil legacy of the state chartered banking system and wildly speculative swings of the economy, the Federal Reserve system seemed a quantum leap forward. Proponents argued that it would restore respectability and stability to the financial system.

In 1913, when the blueprint for the Federal Reserve was created, there were no derivatives, CDOs, or other exotic financial instruments that have become the staples of Wall Street. Change happens so fast on Wall Street that the banking system can't possibly account for it all, and the Fed is constantly playing catch up with time, assuming new powers to react to new crises of every larger dimensions. The Fed is the temple of capitalism ensconced behind firm pillars of respectability. The powers of the Fed impose themselves in myriad ways throughout our entire financial system, but they are ill defined. The Federal Reserve is the lynchpin of the the System," but we know precious little about its operations. What we do know is that the name itself is a misnomer. The Federal Reserve is neither federal nor does it have gold reserves stored in its vault. When the Fed needs to create money, it buys new dollars bills for pennies from the Bureau of Printing and Engraving and then exchanges those crisp dollars with bonds (IOUs) printed by the U. S. Treasury. It is important to note that, technically speaking, the Fed is not an agency of the U. S. Government that is putting money into circulation. The Fed is a privately owned bank like all other commercial banks that create money by making loans.

Here's another imponderable. The Fed is the lender of last resort in the banking system, but where does the Fed get it's funds? Normally the Fed gets its income from interest on U.S government securities it acquires in "open market operations," when it buys Treasuries from bond dealers. But these are not normal times. The needs of the Fed have increased by an order of magnitude in our current crisis. So when the Fed needed $85 billion to lend to insurance giant, AIG for an 80% ownership stake during the peak of the financial crisis, it didn't have enough funds. So what did the Fed do? It turned to the U. S. Treasury. For the first time in history, the U. S. Treasury borrowed the money from investors by issuing Fed bonds, sold in the open market. So the Fed, a private corporation, is borrowing public funds obtained from private investors to prop up private institutions owned by private investors. There's nothing sinister about this, as long as it works. How long can this system sustain itself?

Notice what's happening here. At each stage as private investors get rattled by unstable markets, the Fed steps in to stabilize things using funds borrowed from those private investors.

The Fed's Website says simply, "THE FEDERAL RESERVE IS SUBJECT TO OVERSIGHT BY CONGRESS, WHICH

PERIODICALLY REVIEWS IT'S ACTIVITIES AND CAN ALTER ITS RESPONSIBILITIES BY STATUTE." In other words, if Congress doesn't like what the Fed is doing, all it can do is change the statute.

SECRET FED LOANS GAVE BANKS $13 BILLION UNDISCLOSED TO CONGRESS

THE FEDERAL RESERVE AND THE BIG BANKS FOUGHT FOR MORE THAN TWO YEARS TO KEEP DETAILS OF THE LARGEST BAILOUT IN U.S. HISTORY A SECRET. NOW, THE REST OF THE WORLD CAN SEE WHAT IT WAS MISSING. THE FED DIDN'T TELL ANYONE WHICH BANKS WERE IN TROUBLE SO DEEP THEY REQUIRED A COMBINED $1.2 TRILLION ON DEC. 5, 2008, THEIR SINGLE NEEDIEST DAY. BANKERS DIDN'T MENTION THAT THEY TOOK TENS OF BILLIONS OF DOLLARS IN EMERGENCY LOANS AT THE SAME TIME THEY WERE ASSURING INVESTORS THEIR FIRMS WERE HEALTHY. AND NO ONE CALCULATED UNTIL NOW THAT BANKS REAPED AN ESTIMATED $13 BILLION OF INCOME BY TAKING ADVANTAGE OF THE FED'S BELOW-MARKET RATES, BLOOMBERG MARKETS MAGAZINE REPORTS IN ITS JANUARY ISSUE. SAVED BY THE BAILOUT, BANKERS LOBBIED AGAINST GOVERNMENT REGULATIONS, A JOB MADE EASIER BY THE FED, WHICH NEVER DISCLOSED THE DETAILS OF THE RESCUE TO LAWMAKERS EVEN AS CONGRESS DOLED OUT MORE MONEY AND DEBATED NEW RULES AIMED AT PREVENTING THE NEXT COLLAPSE. A FRESH NARRATIVE OF THE FINANCIAL CRISIS OF 2007 TO 2009 EMERGES FROM 29,000 PAGES OF FED DOCUMENTS OBTAINED UNDER THE FREEDOM OF INFORMATION ACT AND CENTRAL BANK RECORDS OF MORE THAN 21,000 TRANSACTIONS. WHILE FED OFFICIALS SAY THAT ALMOST ALL OF THE LOANS WERE REPAID AND THERE HAVE BEEN NO LOSSES, DETAILS SUGGEST TAXPAYERS PAID A PRICE BEYOND DOLLARS AS THE SECRET FUNDING HELPED PRESERVE A BROKEN STATUS QUO AND ENABLED THE BIGGEST BANKS TO GROW EVEN BIGGER.

BY BOB IVRY, BRADLEY KEOUN AND PHIL KUNTZ · NOV 27, 2011
BLOOMBERG MARKETS MAGAZINE

Who Owns the Federal Reserve?

The Fed is owned by the 12 regional Federal Reserve banks, which are, in turn, owned by member banks of the Federal Reserve System, which are in turn owned by private investors. Shareholders of the Fed receive a 6% dividend on their investment. Not bad. Not great. Because of their charter with the government, Fed member banks can borrow funds either from depositors or from the Fed (The funds rate hovers around 2%). They then lend money to businesses, consumers and government at much higher rates and pocket the difference. This is the essence of banking.

Think about this for a moment. The Fed is entrusted with overseeing the banking system as a lender of last resort, but the Fed is owned by the very same banks that it oversees and extends money to. This leads to some interesting situations, with CEOs of banks also serving on the board of Federal Reserve Banks that advance TARP funds to those banks.

The Fed is by all measures a strange animal and its essential nature is widely misunderstood. When it needs money it creates it out of thin air through electronic entries. All of this is hidden from public view with good reason. The stockholders of the Fed cannot trade their shares of ownership, nor can they pledge them as collateral. When banks join the Federal Reserve System, they are required to buy shares equaling 3% of their capital base. If they fail as banks, their shares are simply returned to the Fed at $100 per share. The board of governors of the 12 regional banks are elected by the member banks, with each bank retaining one vote. Banks are divided into three categories, small, medium and large with each group electing two directors. The President of the United States appoints the Chairperson of the Fed for a four year term, and other directors are appointed by the 12 regional banks for 15 year terms. Thus Congress has virtually no actual authority to review the daily operations of the Fed. It can only amend the charter.

The Cult of Subprime Central Bankers

The world is suffering from the worst downturn since the Great Depression. The crisis has left tens of millions unemployed in the U.S., Europe, and elsewhere. The huge baby boomer generation in the United States, now on the edge of retirement, has seen much of its wealth destroyed with the collapse of the housing bubble.

It would be difficult to imagine a worse economic disaster. Prior periods of bad performance, like the inflation ridden seventies, look like mild flurries compared to the blizzard of bad economic news in which we are now enmeshed.

None of this is new. People don't need economists to tell them that times are bad. However, what the public may not recognize is that the same people who caused this disaster are still calling the shots. Specifically, there has been little change in personnel and no acknowledgment of error at the central banks whose incompetence was responsible for the crisis. Remarkably, this crew of incompetents is still claiming papal infallibility, warning governments and the general public that bad things will happen if they are subjected to more oversight. Instead, the central bankers and their accomplices at the IMF are dictating policies to democratically elected governments. Their agenda seems to be the same everywhere, cut back retirement benefits, reduce public support for health care, weaken unions and make ordinary workers take pay cuts.

Given how much they have messed up, it is amazing that these central bankers have the gall to even show their face in public. They are lucky that they still have jobs -- and very good paying ones at that. (Many of the boys and girls at the IMF can retire with six figure pensions at the age of 50.) Ordinary workers, like teachers, autoworkers, or custodians, would be fired in a second if they performed as badly as the world's central bankers.

Dean Baker
- Co-Director of the Center for Economic and Policy Research

> IF THE AMERICAN PEOPLE KNEW MORE ABOUT THE FED AND HOW IT OPERATES, THEY WOULD BE OUTRAGED.
>
> - WILLIAM GREIDER, AUTHOR,

CONGRESSMAN GRAYSON: WHAT HAVE YOU DONE TO INVESTIGATE THE OFF BALANCE SHEET TRANSACTIONS OF THE FEDERAL RESERVE, WHICH ACCORDING TO BLOOMBERG HAVE INCREASED BY $9 TRILLION, OR $30,000 FOR EVERY MAN WOMAN AND CHILD IN AMERICA, IN THE LAST 8 MONTHS?

INSPECTOR GENERAL COLEMAN: WE HAVE NOT GOTTEN TO A SPECIFIC LEVEL OF DETAIL TO BE ABLE TO RESPOND TO YOUR QUESTION.

CONGRESSMAN GRAYSON: HAVE YOU CONDUCTED AN AUDITING OF THE LOSSES THAT THE FED HAS EXPERIENCED ON IT'S LENDING SINCE LAST SEPTEMBER?

INSPECTOR GENERAL COLEMAN: UNTIL WE ACTUALLY GO OUT AND GATHER THIS INFORMATION, I'M NOT IN A POSITION TO RESPOND TO YOUR QUESTION.

Playing Catch Up With Time

In 1913, when the Federal Reserve System was signed into law, there were no derivatives, CDOs, or other exotic financial instruments that have become the staples of Wall Street. Change happens so fast on Wall Street that regulators and the

Fed can't keep up with it all. The Fed is constantly playing catch up with time, assuming new powers to react to new crises of ever larger dimensions. The Fed is the temple of capitalism ensconced behind firm pillars of respectability. The powers of the Fed impose themselves in myriad ways throughout our entire financial system, but they are ill defined. The Federal Reserve is the lynchpin of "the system," but we know precious little about its operations. We do know is that the name itself is a misnomer. The Federal Reserve is neither federal nor does it have gold reserves stored in its vault. When the Fed needs to create money, it buys new dollars bills for pennies from the Bureau of Printing and Engraving and then exchanges those crisp dollars with bonds (IOUs) printed by the U. S. Treasury. Technically speaking, the Fed is not an agency of the U. S. Government that is putting money into circulation. The Fed is a privately owned bank like all other commercial banks that create money by making loans.

> IT IS TIME TO START NEW BANKS; THE OLD BANKS NEED TO BE COMPLETELY RESTRUCTURED.
> - NIALL FERGUSON

So creating systemic change doesn't mean dismantling banks or the Fed, but it does mean taking a cold, hard look at what aspects of our current system are working and what aspects aren't. We need to make the banking system more responsive to the needs of common people and common purpose. Reopening *The Money Question* is the most economically significant step we can take today. American style capitalism desperately needs to be modernized. The value of our money is entirely a function of confidence in the system, consumer confidence, investor confidence and confidence in the stability of our money. This faith in our money is the basis of all commercial interaction. If we are to think in truly innovative terms about the challenges that await us, we must think about how we can use this all powerful tool we call money, in new ways.

Recently we have developed amazing new tools for the creation of community. Wherever there is a community of trust there can be money. But we have not developed a new form of money that can attach a tangible value to the intangible values inherent in these emerging communities. In our current money and banking system there is a disconnect between the process of wealth creation and the process of value creation. There is a disconnect between value and values. There is a disconnect between money and meaning in our lives. It doesn't have to be like this. There is a better way to integrate money with meaning and value with values.

> IF CONGRESS HAS THE RIGHT UNDER THE CONSTITUTION TO ISSUE PAPER MONEY, IT WAS GIVEN TO BE USED BY THEMSELVES, NOT TO BE DELEGATED TO INDIVIDUALS OR CORPORATIONS.
>
> - PRESIDENT ANDREW JACKSON

For almost a hundred years we have been working with the same monetary and banking system, despite a radically altered landscape of business and society. The time has come to move beyond the rhetoric about new regulation and move towards a sustainable solution to our money and banking crisis that can harness the inherent good within each of us and channel it towards the common good. Our current crisis forces us to think anew. We don't need to replace our existing money and banking system, but rather to let the evolution of the system continue.

If big banks assume too much risk, let them suffer the consequences–by letting some fail and letting others dispose of assets in an orderly manner. In place of the concentrated big banks, let a complementary "cloud" banking system grow from the bottom up. Let a dynamic system grow and evolve as new dimensions are added by new participants. These smaller decentralized public and Social Banks will moderate the instabilities, and imbalances of the current system. Because it is dynamic, it has the potential to awaken the economy and catalyze a new wave of wealth creation throughout our society over time by creating mechanisms to measure, manage and monetize the value of what current markets do not measure or recognize. The value of this currently recognized value in our society is estimated by economists to be more than $2 trillion. That could be a powerful stimulus to a slumbering economy, if we can find a way to monetize it. This is what this book is about.

> THE DOLLAR'S ROLE AS A GOOD STORE OF VALUE IS QUESTIONABLE AND THE CURRENCY HAS A HIGH DEGREE OF RISK. ... THE GLOBAL FINANCIAL CRISIS SIGNALS THE FAILURE OF AMERICAN-STYLE CAPITALISM,
>
> - NOBEL PRIZE-WINNING ECONOMIST JOSEPH STIGLITZ.

Now in the midst of the most serious financial crisis of our lifetime, there are many good reasons to reconsider "*The Money Question.*" Our current money system is outdated and outmoded. Our banking system is blind to the needs of entire sectors of the economy. It concentrates power in the hands of Wall Street bankers who are solely interested in reaping profits from their power to create money. That system is not working well. It's time for another wave of systemic innovation: the democratization of the power to create money through the introduction of a parallel system of public and Social Banks. To insure that the overall supply of money was stabilized, some of the existing commercial banks will be allowed to fail or be reduced in size. They will be held accountable for the imprudent risks they have taken. Surviving banks will be required to hold greater reserves to stabilize the system. New liquidity to the system will be provided by newer, smaller social and public purpose banks. The whole system will be more stable and equitable.

BANKING WAS CONCEIVED IN INIQUITY AND WAS BORN IN SIN. THE BANKERS OWN THE EARTH. TAKE IT AWAY FROM THEM, BUT LEAVE THEM THE POWER TO CREATE DEPOSITS, AND WITH THE FLICK OF THE PEN THEY WILL CREATE ENOUGH DEPOSITS TO BUY IT BACK AGAIN. HOWEVER, TAKE IT AWAY FROM THEM, AND ALL THE GREAT FORTUNES LIKE MINE WILL DISAPPEAR AND THEY OUGHT TO DISAPPEAR, FOR THIS WOULD BE A HAPPIER AND BETTER WORLD TO LIVE IN. BUT, IF YOU WISH TO REMAIN THE SLAVES OF BANKERS AND PAY THE COST OF YOUR OWN SLAVERY, LET THEM CONTINUE TO CREATE DEPOSITS.

- BY SIR JOSIAH STAMP

We don't have to accept a system that creates an economic chasm between Wall Street and Main Street. We don't have to accept a system that exacerbates income inequalities, and creates two classes of people: those with economic and political access and those without it. That economic divide forms at the point of origin of credit in our banking system. Those on one side of the divide have been empowered to create money and become the masters. Those on the other side are in perpetual need of borrowed funds and they are the slaves. This is the nature of our modern money and banking system. It's an answer to *The Money Question* that was developed by an elite group of bankers acting their own self interest over 100 years ago. It goes unchallenged and unquestioned, despite it's fundamental flaws, instabilities and inequities. The flawed answer to *The Money Question* we're living with, lies at the heart of our current economic and financial crisis.

THERE IS A BETTER WAY: ONE THAT DOESN'T FAVOR OF WALL STREET SO HEAVILY. THE BETTER ANSWER IS A BANKING SYSTEM THAT IS NOT EXCLUSIVELY DEBT BASED AND WHERE NO BANK IS "TOO BIG TO FAIL." A SIMPLE SHIFT IN THINKING WILL CHANGE EVERYTHING AND INSPIRE HOPE FOR MILLIONS OF AMERICANS WHO NOW DESPAIR OF THEIR ECONOMIC FUTURE.

Fed Feeding Frenzy

When the Fed needs money it creates it out of thin air through electronic entries. All of this is hidden from public view with good reason.

WALL STREET PROFITS FROM TRADES WITH FED

WALL STREET BANKS ARE REAPING OUTSIZED PROFITS BY TRADING WITH THE FEDERAL RESERVE, RAISING QUESTIONS ABOUT WHETHER THE CENTRAL BANK IS DRIVING HARD ENOUGH BARGAINS IN ITS DEALINGS WITH PRIVATE SECTOR COUNTERPARTIES, OFFICIALS AND INDUSTRY EXECUTIVES SAY. THE FED HAS EMERGED AS ONE OF WALL STREET'S BIGGEST CUSTOMERS DURING THE FINANCIAL CRISIS, BUYING MASSIVE AMOUNTS OF SECURITIES TO HELP STABILISE THE MARKETS. IN SOME CASES, SUCH AS THE MARKET FOR MORTGAGE-BACKED SECURITIES, THE FED BUYS MORE BONDS THAN ANY OTHER PARTY. HOWEVER, THE FED IS NOT A TYPICAL MARKET PLAYER. IN THE INTERESTS OF TRANSPARENCY, IT OFTEN ANNOUNCES ITS INTENTION TO BUY PARTICULAR SECURITIES IN ADVANCE. A FORMER FED OFFICIAL SAID THIS STRATEGY ENABLES BANKS TO SELL THESE SECURITIES TO THE FED AT AN INFLATED PRICE. THE RESULTING PROFITS REPRESENT A RELATIVELY HIDDEN FORM OF SUPPORT FOR BANKS, AND WALL STREET HAS GEARED UP TO TAKE ADVANTAGE.

- HENNY SENDER. THE FINANCIAL TIMES: AUGUST 2, 2009

The Fed is entrusted with overseeing the banking system as a lender of last resort, but the Fed is owned by the very same banks that it oversees and extends money to. This leads to some interesting situations, with CEOs of banks also serving on the board of Federal Reserve Banks that advance TARP funds to those banks. At a minimum, the lack of transparency and dual roles played by some members of these exclusive boards leaves the door open to self dealing.

Take the example of Jaime Dimon, CEO of JP Morgan Chase. At the peak of the financial crisis in September 2008, Dimon acting as Chase CEO, negotiated a deal brokered by the New York Fed to buy Bear Stears stock for pennies on the dollar. But Dimon also sits on the Board of Directors of the New York Fed.

A conflict of interest? Perhaps nothing improper occurs behind closed doors, but the legal possibility is left open for a private club of exclusive bankers to operate without an adequate measure of public oversight and make private agreements that clearly benefit its members. What really happens in the secrecy of the Fed's chambers?

Where Does the Fed Get its Funds?

Here's another imponderable. The Fed is the lender of last resort in the banking system, but where does the Fed get it's funds? Normally the Fed gets its income from interest on U.S government securities it acquires in "open market operations," when it buys Treasuries from bond dealers. But these are not normal times. The needs of the Fed have increased by an order of magnitude in our current crisis. So when the Fed needed $85 billion to lend to insurance giant, AIG for an 80% ownership stake last fall, it didn't have enough funds. So what did the Fed do? It turned to the U. S. Treasury. For the first time in history, the U. S. Treasury borrowed the money from investors by issuing Fed bonds, sold in the open market. So the Fed, a private corporation, is borrowing public funds obtained from private investors to prop up private institutions owned by private investors. There's nothing sinister about this, as long as it works. How long can this system sustain itself?

Notice what's happening here. At each stage as private investors get rattled by unstable markets, the Fed steps in to stabilize things using funds borrowed from those private investors. Why do investors trust a government that is now over $11 trillion in debt? They do so because they trust the system. They do so because they believe that at some point the government will pay them back. But the government keeps borrowing more and more–this year adding $1.6 trillion to the national debt this year, $1.4 trillion next year and $9 trillion over the next 10 years. At what point does the system itself start to look unstable?

> # GIVE ME CONTROL OF A NATION'S MONEY AND I CARE NOT WHO MAKES THE LAWS.
>
> ## - MAYER AMSCHEL ROTHSCHILD

Is Trust in the System Well Placed?

THERE IS NOTHING BUT TRUST IN THE SYSTEM BACKING UP THE $10 TRILLION IN CURRENCY THAT CIRCULATES AS THE LIFEBLOOD OF OUR ECONOMY.

Our current money system is governed by a paradox–a paradox so powerful in its simplicity that few of us ever give it a thought. The paradox is this:

OUR MONEY HAS NO INTRINSIC VALUE. THE VALUE OF OUR MONEY IS ENTIRELY A FUNCTION OF THE TRUST WE PLACE IN THE SYSTEM THAT SUPPORTS IT. IF THIS TRUST DISSIPATES TO A POINT OF RECKONING, A COLLAPSE IN THE SYSTEM THAT SUPPORTS OUR MONEY IS INEVITABLE.

We got a glimpse of that reckoning on September 18, 2008, when Treasury Secretary Paulson and Federal Reserve Chair Bernanke assembled leaders from Congress and presented them with a stark analysis. The banking system had seized up. Of the five major investment banks, all were deemed technically insolvent. Their liabilities exceeded their assets and the gap between them was accelerating at an alarming rate. Lehman Brothers had already failed, completely wiping out billions in shareholder value almost overnight. Three others were in danger of failing if immediate action was not taken. The mood in that meeting was tense.

Can Debt Continue to Grow Indefinitely?

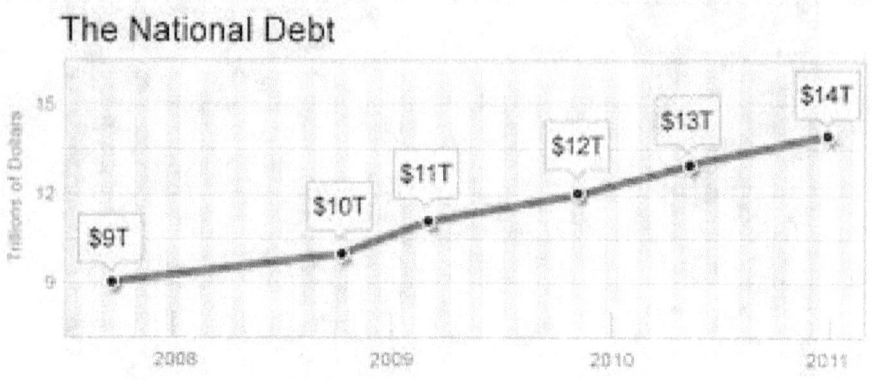

The National Debt

Over the last 30 years we have experienced an explosive increase of both public and private debt to levels unprecedented in human history. The economy has expanded by borrowing increasingly and hoping the future will bring continued growth to support even more debt. Corporate debt is now over $46 trillion and companies all across the spectrum are desperate for additional capital. Between 1980 and the present, the U. S. national debt has increased 1200% from roughly $1 trillion to almost $15 trillion. In the 1980s credit card balances increased 400% and credit card spending increased 500%. By 2007 consumer debt had reached $2.57 trillion. Charge-off rates on credit cards rose to an all-time high of 10.76% in June 2009 - meaning that card companies have given up hope on collecting nearly 11% of their balances, on an annualized basis. A year ago, the charge-off rate was 6.46%.

Have We All Been Swindled?

In its depth and suddenness, the U.S. economic and financial crisis is shockingly reminiscent of moments we have recently seen in emerging markets (and only in emerging markets): South Korea (1997), Malaysia (1998), Russia and Argentina (time and again). In each of those cases, global investors, afraid that the country or its financial sector wouldn't be able to pay off mountainous debt, suddenly stopped lending. And in each case, that fear became self-fulfilling, as banks that couldn't roll over their debt did, in fact, become unable to pay. This is precisely what drove Lehman Brothers into bankruptcy on September 15, causing all sources of funding to the U.S. financial sector to dry up overnight. Just as in emerging-market crises, the weakness in the banking system has quickly rippled out into the rest of the economy, causing a severe economic contraction and hardship for millions of people. ... But there's a deeper and more disturbing similarity: elite business interests—financiers, in the case of the U.S.—played a central role in creating the crisis, making ever-larger gambles, with the implicit backing of the government, until the inevitable collapse. More alarming, they are now using their influence to prevent precisely the sorts of reforms that are needed, and fast, to pull the economy out of its nosedive. The government seems helpless, or unwilling, to act against them.

- Simon Johnson, The Quiet Coup, The Atlantic, May 2009

With the arrival of securitization, massive trading operations, derivatives, CDOs and other complex financial instruments, Wall Street bankers have been transformed from conservative lenders into high rollers and risk takers. The big Wall Street banks take these risks, because they know that President Obama, Ben Bernanke, Tim Geitner and others have made it clear that the government will do whatever it takes to keep the current system afloat no matter how much of the taxpayer's dollars is put at risk with bailouts, guarantees and back room deals between the Fed, the U. S. Treasury and the big banks. The governments current commitments now clock in at $12.8 trillion to keep the current system afloat.

Bonds: Next Bubble Burst?

"What's that hiss? Bond sales break record, but "investors" demand higher yields...U.S. budget deficit sets annual record... in just 4 months! Key trading signals from one of our resident options analysts... Data still disappoint... housing, jobs, retail improve slightly, but still in the dumps... Last, Dubai in danger... foreigners flee so hurriedly they're leaving cars behind... The U.S. treasury broke two bond sale records this week: Uncle Sam sold $21 billion in 10-year notes Tuesday and another $14 billion in 30-year bonds yesterday — both all-time daily highs. Both are just small pieces of the expected $2 trillion in U.S. debt sales this year... at least." [4]

> *The largest Asian central banks have gone on record that they are curbing their purchases of US debt. And they are also diversifying their huge reserves, steadily moving away from the dollar. The risks have simply become too many and too serious."*
> *— W. Joseph Stroupe, Editor, Global Events*

But bond investors are finally starting to see the forest for the trees. The yield on those 10 years climbed above 3% this week, the highest level in more than three months. "Except for U.S. Treasuries, what can you hold?" lamented Luo Ping, the director of China's Banking Regulatory Commission. In a speech in New York yesterday, Luo said China will continue to buy and hold U.S. Treasuries. With a giant tone of reservation: "You don't hold Japanese government bonds or U.K. bonds. U.S. Treasuries are the safe haven. For everyone, including China, it is the only option. "We hate you guys," Mr. Luo said, half kidding after his speech. "Once you start issuing $1-2 trillion... we know the dollar is going to depreciate, so we hate you guys, but there is nothing much we can do.

---

4 : Financial News, Feb 13, 2009 I By Addison Wiggin I Category

Increasing Income Inequality

At the most fundamental level, the root cause of our financial crisis is that our economic system is propelled by a dynamic of increasing imbalances between those who create wealth and those who create value for our society. Those with financial power and credibility tend to have greater access to debt and equity capital markets than those without such credibility and power. As a result, they are able to enhance their economic stature by creating wealth through increasingly exotic and highly leveraged financial instruments. But are these wizards creating value to society?

While this happens, the economic stature of those at the bottom of the economic ladder is diminished as they struggle to survive. They dig themselves deeper and deeper into a mountain of debt until many default on their mortgages, credit cards or consumer loans. We have learned to our dismay that it only takes a small number of borrowers defaulting on their mortgages to destabilize the entire system. This is the nature of highly leveraged systems. Numerous studies have documented how the dynamics of our economic system tend to exacerbate economic inequalities. But the numbers of people and groups that are being left behind by the economic system has grown so large that the entire system has become destabilized.

> *Essentially, Americans had migrated from one society to another — from a society of high trust to a society of low trust, from a society of optimism to a society of foreboding, from a society in which certain financial habits applied to a society in which they did not.*
> *- February 13, 2009, The New York Times,*

Today, the system has clearly grown out of balance. Main Street consumers are paying usurious rates interest on their credit card balances, while Wall Street banks borrow funds at abnormally low interest rates. Exacerbating the imbalances, these banks receive billions of dollars in taxpayer funded bailouts. Why? Because they have jeopardized the stability of our financial system by extending risky mortgages to subprime borrowers without ever verifying their creditworthiness. The real income of Main Street workers is declining, while Wall Street bonuses are flowing again, despite all the political rhetoric about cutting executive compensation.

Legislation By Lobbyists

The down payment on Wall Street's influence begins with campaign contributions. It extends through the revolving door that connects the Wall Street–Washington corridor and is consolidated through the promulgation of a belief system that supports the widely accepted, but dubious, credo, *"What's good for Wall Street is good for America."* In less developed economies and emerging nations this sort of dealing is often conducted through bribe. In America, we are more civilized. Massive looting of government coffers is rendered legal, through U. S. Treasury sponsored bailouts, back room deals of the Fed and Congressionally mandated stimulus packages. Much of this money has not been accounted for.

(Illustration: James T. Pendergrast)

> *... Senate Majority Whip Richard Durbin of Illinois unsuccessfully fought for a congressional amendment he said will have helped 1.7 million Americans save their homes from foreclosure, the senator told a radio station back home that, "The banks - hard to believe in a time when we're facing a banking crisis that many of the banks created - are still the most powerful lobby on Capitol Hill. And they frankly own the place. He can say the same of the White House.*
> *- Bill Moyers and Michael Winship*

The close personal and business relationships between high ranking officials in the banking industry and the Treasury only makes this situation more comfortable for the bankers. This is a win/win situation for the bankers and a lose/lose situation for the taxpayers. It's the inevitable result of a system where power is concentrated in a few mega-banks that are deemed "too big to fail" by the government.

Banks step up spending on lobbying to fight proposed stiffer regulations

Even as the financial industry has sought to keep a low public profile, some of the country's largest banks have ramped up their spending on lobbying to fight off some of the stiffest regulatory proposals pending in Congress. Lobbying expenditures jumped 12% from 2008 to $29.8 million last year among the eight banks and private equity firms that spent the most to influence legislation, according to data compiled from disclosure forms filed with Congress.

The biggest spender was JPMorgan Chase & Co., whose lobbying budget rose 12% to $6.2 million, enough for the firm to have more than 30 lobbyists working for it. Among other banks, spending on lobbying rose 27% at Wells Fargo & Co. and 16% at Morgan Stanley.

By Nathaniel Popper, February 16, 2010, The Los Angeles Times - http://www.latimes.com/business/la-fi-bank-lobbying16-2010feb16,0,1048819,print.story?igoogle=1

I have never seen such a scrum of bank lobbyists as I have in the last year -- and I've worked on quite a few bank issues over the years. ... It seems like everybody is out of work except for bank lobbyists.

-Ed Mierzwinski - U.S. Public Interest Research Group

Too Big to Fail is Too Big

Fifteen years ago, the combined assets of our six biggest banks totaled 17 percent of our GDP. By 2006, that number was 55 percent. Right now, it stands at 63 percent.

• The big four have half of the market for mortgages and two-thirds of the market for credit cards.
• Five banks have over 95 percent of the market for over-the-counter derivatives. Three U.S. banks have over 40 percent of the global market for stock underwriting.

The government created the mega-giants (they are not the product of free market competition), and their very size destroys the real economy like a massive black hole destroys the matter around it. The very size of the giant banks enables them to easily capture politicians.
– Simon Johnson · Author · 13 Bankers

Niall Ferguson on Debt and National Security

Call the United States what you like—superpower, hegemon, or empire—but its ability to manage its finances is closely tied to its ability to remain the predominant global military power... This is how empires decline. It begins with a debt explosion. It ends with an inexorable reduction in the resources available for the Army, Navy, and Air Force...

If the United States doesn't come up soon with a credible plan to restore the federal budget to balance over the next five to 10 years, the danger is very real that a debt crisis could lead to a major weakening of American power. The precedents are certainly there. Habsburg Spain defaulted on all or part of its debt 14 times between 1557 and 1696 and also succumbed to inflation due to a surfeit of New World silver. Prerevolutionary France was spending 62 percent of royal revenue on debt service by 1788. The Ottoman Empire went the same way: interest payments and amortization rose from 15 percent of the budget in 1860 to 50 percent in 1875. And don't forget the last great English-speaking empire. By the interwar years, interest payments were consuming 44 percent of the British budget, making it intensely difficult to rearm in the face of a new German threat.

Call it the fatal arithmetic of imperial decline. Without radical fiscal reform, it could apply to America next.
... Spain was the first global superpower...With Spain as its political base, and gold and silver flowing in from its American colonies, the Hapsburg dynasty became the dominant power in Europe. It controlled rich parts of Italy through Naples and Milan, and Central Europe from the Netherlands through the Holy Roman Empire to Austria....

The Hapsburgs went into decline in the 17th century, and while any such momentous event has many causes, for our purposes the focus will be on the economic collapse of Spain, which not only sapped the empire of strength but served to build up the power of its rivals.

The demands of empire required a strong and growing economy, but Spain did not keep up with the economic expansion that was taking place in other parts of Europe. Madrid's financial base fell out from under its empire. Spain could continue to consume in the short term because of the flow of precious metals from American mines, but it could not produce the goods it needed at home, which in the long-run proved fatal to its standing as a Great Power and as an advanced society.

The Banking Cartels

Banks operate a legalized cartel that gives them monopolist power to create our currency. Here's how the current system works. You make a deposit of $1000 at your local bank. If your bank is like most banks, it has a fractional reserve ratio of 10 to 1. This means that for each $1000 the bank holds on deposit, it can lend ten times that amount. So if the bank holds your entire $1000 on deposit, they can extend credit of $10,000. Where did the bank get the additional $9000? Did they have it in a vault someplace? No, the bank simply created it, with accounting entries. In the process, $9000 has been introduced to our financial system? Presto, $9000 is magically created by the bank, because this is what our fractional reserve banking system empowers them to do. The process doesn't stop there. That $10,000 in credit flows through the financial system and some of it gets deposited at other banks. Those banks then use those funds as deposits to make more loans. So it goes.

"BANKS ACTUALLY CREATE MONEY WHEN THEY LEND IT. HERE'S HOW IT WORKS: MOST OF A BANK'S LOANS ARE MADE TO ITS OWN CUSTOMERS AND ARE DEPOSITED IN THEIR CHECKING ACCOUNTS. BECAUSE THE LOAN BECOMES A NEW DEPOSIT, JUST LIKE A PAYCHECK DOES, THE BANK . . . HOLDS A SMALL PERCENTAGE OF THAT NEW AMOUNT IN RESERVE AND AGAIN LENDS THE REMAINDER TO SOMEONE ELSE, REPEATING THE MONEY-CREATION PROCESS MANY TIMES."

- ON THE WEBSITE OF THE FEDERAL RESERVE BANK OF DALLAS
   HTTP://WWW.DALLASFED.ORG/EDUCATE/EVERYDAY/EV9.HTML

WHAT IS BACKING UP THE $10 TRILLION DOLLARS IN MONEY THAT FLOWS THROUGHOUT THE FINANCIAL SYSTEM? NOTHING! NOTHING, BUT TRUST BASED UPON A SIGNATURE ON A LOAN AGREEMENT AND COLLATERAL OF UNCERTAIN VALUE, BACKS UP THE 10 TRILLION DOLLARS THAT ARE THE LIFEBLOOD OF OUR ECONOMY.

The way money is created defines how economic power is distributed in society. Meanwhile Wall Street bankers receive bailouts and fat green bonuses, while Main Street workers receive default notices and thin pink slips.

BREAK THE OLIGARCHY
OF THE BIG BANKS

BIG BANKS, IT SEEMS, HAVE ONLY GAINED POLITICAL STRENGTH SINCE THE CRISIS BEGAN. AND THIS IS NOT SURPRISING. WITH THE FINANCIAL SYSTEM SO FRAGILE, THE DAMAGE THAT A MAJOR BANK FAILURE COULD CAUSE—LEHMAN WAS SMALL RELATIVE TO CITIGROUP OR BANK OF AMERICA—IS MUCH GREATER THAN IT WOULD BE DURING ORDINARY TIMES. THE BANKS HAVE BEEN EXPLOITING THIS FEAR AS THEY WRING FAVORABLE DEALS OUT OF WASHINGTON. ... AT THE ROOT OF THE BANKS' PROBLEMS ARE THE LARGE LOSSES THEY HAVE UNDOUBTEDLY TAKEN ON THEIR SECURITIES AND LOAN PORTFOLIOS. BUT THEY DON'T WANT TO RECOGNIZE THE FULL EXTENT OF THEIR LOSSES, BECAUSE THAT WOULD LIKELY EXPOSE THEM AS INSOLVENT. SO THEY TALK DOWN THE PROBLEM, AND ASK FOR HANDOUTS THAT AREN'T ENOUGH TO MAKE THEM HEALTHY (AGAIN, THEY CAN'T REVEAL THE SIZE OF THE HANDOUTS THAT WOULD BE NECESSARY FOR THAT), BUT ARE ENOUGH TO KEEP THEM UPRIGHT A LITTLE LONGER. THIS BEHAVIOR IS CORROSIVE: UNHEALTHY BANKS EITHER DON'T LEND (HOARDING MONEY TO SHORE UP RESERVES) OR THEY MAKE DESPERATE GAMBLES ON HIGH-RISK LOANS AND INVESTMENTS THAT COULD PAY OFF BIG, BUT PROBABLY WON'T PAY OFF AT ALL. IN EITHER CASE, THE ECONOMY SUFFERS FURTHER, AND AS IT DOES, BANK ASSETS THEMSELVES CONTINUE TO DETERIORATE—CREATING A HIGHLY DESTRUCTIVE VICIOUS CYCLE. ... TO BREAK THIS CYCLE, THE GOVERNMENT MUST FORCE THE BANKS TO ACKNOWLEDGE THE SCALE OF THEIR PROBLEMS. ... UNDER THESE CONDITIONS, CLEANING UP BANK BALANCE SHEETS IS IMPOSSIBLE.... BUT ONLY DECISIVE GOVERNMENT ACTION—EXPOSING THE FULL EXTENT OF THE FINANCIAL ROT AND RESTORING SOME SET OF BANKS TO PUBLICLY VERIFIABLE HEALTH—CAN CURE THE FINANCIAL SECTOR AS A WHOLE. ... BUT IN FACT, WHILE NECESSARY, IT IS INSUFFICIENT. THE SECOND PROBLEM THE U.S. FACES—THE POWER OF THE OLIGARCHY—IS JUST AS IMPORTANT AS THE IMMEDIATE CRISIS OF LENDING. AND THE ADVICE FROM THE IMF ON THIS FRONT WOULD AGAIN BE SIMPLE: BREAK THE OLIGARCHY. ... OVERSIZE INSTITUTIONS DISPROPORTIONATELY INFLUENCE PUBLIC POLICY; THE MAJOR BANKS WE HAVE TODAY DRAW MUCH OF THEIR POWER FROM BEING TOO BIG TO FAIL.

- SIMON JOHNSON, THE QUIET COUP, THE ATLANTIC, MAY 2009
HTTP://WWW.THEATLANTIC.COM/DOC/200905/IMF-ADVICE

Destruction Through Derivatives

"According to the Bank of International Settlements: The derivatives market is leveraged at 38 to 1. That is to say that $8.3 trillion of real money is controlling $313 trillion in derivatives. That's leverage. These figures are just for the over - the - counter derivatives and do not include the global exchange traded derivatives in currencies, stocks and commodities which are another $75 trillion." "$8.3 trillion of

real money is controlling $313 trillion in derivatives!" This illustrates the sheer magnitude of the problem and the economy-busting potential of a miscalculation. That's why Warren Buffett calls derivatives "weapons of mass destruction". If there's a fire-sale in hedge funds or derivatives, there's nothing the Plunge Protection Team or the Federal Reserve will be able to do to stop a meltdown. The market will crash leaving nothing behind. We are reaping the rewards of a lawless, deregulated system which has removed all the safeguards for protecting the small investor. There is no government oversight; it's a joke. The stock market is a crap-shoot that serves the sole interests of establishment elites, corporate plutocrats, and banking giants. The small investor is trapped beneath the wheel and getting squeezed more and more every day. He has no way to fix the markets like the big guys and no lobby to promote his interests. He must arrive at his decisions by researching publicly available information and then plunking down his money. That's it. He'd be better off in a casino; the odds are about the same. Easy money almost everywhere leads to leverage and speculation. No where is this more prevalent than in the global derivatives market. It is not out of the question that third party defaults and risk aversion designed instruments that collapse and go sour may someday overwhelm the financial markets." [5]

---

[5] Mike Whitney's Blog: http://www.smirkingchimp.com/author/mike_whitney

Debt Denial To The Tune of $15 Trillion

Wall Street relies on the government, but the government has now gone almost $12 trillion in debt. In the last year alone, the obligations of the Fed, the Treasury Department and the FDIC top out at an additional $11.7 trillion.

MOUNTAIN OF DEBT:
RISING DEBT MAY BE NEXT CRISIS

THE DEBT GAP IS "SOMETHING THAT KEEPS ME AWAKE AT NIGHT," OBAMA SAYS. HE PLEDGED TO CUT THE BUDGET "DEFICIT" ROUGHLY IN HALF BY THE END OF HIS FIRST TERM. BUT "DEFICIT" JUST MEANS THE DIFFERENCE BETWEEN GOVERNMENT RECEIPTS AND SPENDING IN A SINGLE BUDGET YEAR. THIS YEAR'S DEFICIT IS NOW ESTIMATED AT ABOUT $1.85 TRILLION. DEFICITS DON'T REFLECT HOLDOVER INDEBTEDNESS FROM PREVIOUS YEARS. SOME SPENDING ITEMS — SUCH AS EMERGENCY APPROPRIATIONS BILLS AND RECEIPTS IN THE SOCIAL SECURITY PROGRAM — AREN'T INCLUDED, EITHER, ALTHOUGH THEY ARE PART OF THE NATIONAL DEBT. THE NATIONAL DEBT IS A BROADER, AND MORE TELLING, WAY TO LOOK AT THE GOVERNMENT'S BALANCE SHEETS THAN GLANCING AT DEFICITS. ACCORDING TO THE TREASURY DEPARTMENT, WHICH UPDATES THE NUMBER "TO THE PENNY" EVERY FEW DAYS, THE NATIONAL DEBT WAS $11,518,472,742,288 ON WEDNESDAY, JULY 1ST ... THE OVERALL DEBT IS NOW SLIGHTLY OVER 80 PERCENT OF THE ANNUAL OUTPUT OF THE ENTIRE U.S. ECONOMY, AS MEASURED BY THE GROSS DOMESTIC PRODUCT.

- TOM RAUM – WASHINGTON (AP) - JULY 3, 2009
HTTP://WWW.GOOGLE.COM/HOSTEDNEWS/AP/ARTICLE/
ALEQM5GASX8F19RPP2PFUHGRCOJ9CQBRDWD99723A8O

Why do investors trust a government that is now over $15 trillion in debt? They do so because they trust the system. They do so because they believe that at some point the government will pay them back. But the government keeps borrowing more and more–this year adding $1.6 trillion to the national debt this year, $1.4 trillion next year and $9 trillion over the next 10 years. At what point does the system itself start to look unstable? Who is looking taking a look at the longer term implications of all the borrowing of the Fed and U. S. Treasury?

It's a system that for all its imperfections was always better than any alternative people can think of; but little by little, the failings of the system have been magnified. The volatility of financial markets has been growing. The scale and sophistication of swindling has increased to the point of high drama. While the rollers and risk takers dominate the Wall Street landscape, the real economy on Main Street is stagnating. In the last decade, *The New York Times* recently reported, the overall economy has added no new jobs. This is the first time since the Great Depression that this has happened. Manufacturing continued has continued it long decline in the United States, with only modest gains in retailing and service sectors.

THE HARSH REALITY THAT IS BEING REPRESSED IS THIS: THE WESTERN WORLD IS SUFFERING A CRISIS OF EXCESSIVE INDEBTEDNESS. MANY GOVERNMENTS ARE TOO HIGHLY LEVERAGED, AS ARE MANY CORPORATIONS. MORE IMPORTANTLY, HOUSEHOLDS ARE GROANING UNDER UNPRECEDENTED DEBT BURDENS. AVERAGE HOUSEHOLD SECTOR DEBT HAS REACHED 141 PER CENT OF DISPOSABLE INCOME IN THE UNITED STATES AND 177 PER CENT IN THE UNITED KINGDOM. WORST OF ALL ARE THE BANKS. SOME OF THE BEST-KNOWN NAMES IN AMERICAN AND EUROPEAN FINANCE HAVE BALANCE SHEETS FORTY, SIXTY OR EVEN A HUNDRED TIMES THE SIZE OF THEIR CAPITAL. AVERAGE U.S. INVESTMENT BANK LEVERAGE WAS ABOVE 25 TO 1 AT THE END OF 2008. EUROZONE BANK LEVERAGE WAS MORE THAN 30 TO 1. BRITISH BANK BALANCE SHEETS ARE EQUAL TO A STAGGERING 440 PER CENT OF GROSS DOMESTIC PRODUCT. THE DELUSION THAT A CRISIS OF EXCESS DEBT CAN BE SOLVED BY CREATING MORE DEBT IS AT THE HEART OF THE GREAT REPRESSION. YET THAT IS PRECISELY WHAT MOST GOVERNMENTS CURRENTLY PROPOSE TO DO.

- NIALL FERGUSON

Is it any wonder then, that so many people, companies, governments now find themselves under the crushing burden of interest and principle repayments. We fail to realize that much of the financial stress in our lives is inevitable given the way money is created in our current economic system–as debt–magically made real by financial wizards who are constantly blending new concoctions of lending and leverage. Most of us tend to view the world of finance through the lens of our own situation-seldom considering the systemic imperatives that create a certain inevitability to the crushing burden of debt in our lives.

So what must we do now to stabilize the system? Regulatory reform has it's limitations because clever lawyers can always devise ways around laws and regulatory agencies tend to become captive of the sectors they are supposed to regulate. Laws enacted in earlier times are inadequate to deal with the scale and complexity of our current crisis. During crises there is a push towards increased oversight, but as crises subside and fade from public consciousness, the political forces are arrayed against regulation. Already, the political power of Wall Street is being mobilized to weaken what he proposes.

Doing nothing is not an option. Without social innovation and change, we are all headed towards a future of continued instabilities, wild swings in confidence, eroding trust in the system and eventually the collapse of the dollar and the institutions upon which a stable currency is based. When these institutions start failing, their collapse will be seen as obvious—as obvious as the collapse of credit markets and the meltdown of the real estate market.

> ## MORE EMPIRES HAVE FALLEN BECAUSE OF RECKLESS FINANCES THAN INVASION.
> ## - GEORGE WASHINGTON

Call the United States what you like—superpower, hegemon, or empire—but its ability to manage its finances is closely tied to its ability to remain the predominant global military power...

This is how empires decline. It begins with a debt explosion. It ends with an inexorable reduction in the resources available for the Army, Navy, and Air Force...

If the United States doesn't come up soon with a credible plan to restore the federal budget to balance over the next five to 10 years, the danger is very real that a debt crisis could lead to a major weakening of American power.

The precedents are certainly there. Habsburg Spain defaulted on all or part of its debt 14 times between 1557 and 1696 and also succumbed to inflation due to a surfeit of New World silver. Prerevolutionary France was spending 62 percent of royal revenue on debt service by 1788. The Ottoman Empire went the same way: interest payments and amortization rose from 15 percent of the budget in 1860 to 50 percent in 1875. And don't forget the last great English-speaking empire. By the interwar years, interest payments were consuming 44 percent of the British budget, making it intensely difficult to rearm in the face of a new German threat.

Call it the fatal arithmetic of imperial decline. Without radical fiscal reform, it could apply to America next.

- Niall Ferguson, Harvard Professor

Occupy Wall Street: Not Here To Destroy Capitalism, But To Remind Us Who Saved It

There are a lot of ways to tell the story about how the world was saved, but the Occupy Wall Street is starting to remind the world of one narrative in particular. When everything seemed ready to collapse, there was one group of people left in this world who had enough cred on the street to save the day -- the American taxpayers. They were the only people left in whom anyone would put their full faith and credit as a sure thing. And it's easy to see why, seeing as they had built the greatest nation on earth out of their combined blood, sweat and tears.

It was the American taxpayers who went to war, on everyone's behalf, with that dread cobra, and they sacrificed $4.7 trillion of their own money to bring everyone back from the brink. That's $4.7 trillion that the American taxpayer willingly parted with, money that could have been put to any other priority. There's still about a trillion and half that hasn't even been returned -- but that's not where our focus should be. Our focus should be on the other scars left by that sacrifice. A massive unemployment crisis, people being kicked out of their homes, college graduates leaving their institutions of higher learning without a clear grasp on a future and saddled with debt (because that's what they were told to do to get ahead in this world) -- that's where our focus should have been, but wasn't, until those folks started gathering in the streets.

Three years later, if you even allude to that sacrifice, you still elicit from all sides the cry of "class warfare." And I'll admit, it's a pretty seductive metaphor. Not long ago, my counter to that charge was to point out that the Occupiers were an encampment of casualties and refugees from the last class war. But I've since realized that while this is a good, glib line, the politics are too convenient. In reality, the people of Occupy Wall Street are the people who fought the last war on everyone's behalf. They are a neglected band of veterans from the Battle To Save The Global Economy. They're attempting to remind America that we all fought on the same side.

by Jason Linkins - http://www.huffingtonpost.com/2011/10/27/occupy-wall-street-isnt-h_n_1035988.html

Populist Manifesto No. 1

POETS, COME OUT OF YOUR CLOSETS,
OPEN YOUR <u>WINDOWS</u>, OPEN YOUR DOORS,
YOU HAVE BEEN HOLED-UP TOO LONG
IN YOUR CLOSED WORLDS. ...

NO TIME NOW FOR THE ARTIST TO HIDE
ABOVE, BEYOND, <u>BEHIND THE SCENES</u>,
INDIFFERENT, PARING HIS <u>FINGERNAILS</u>,
REFINING HIMSELF OUT OF EXISTENCE. ...

THE HOUR OF OMING IS OVER,
THE TIME OF KEENING COME,
A TIME FOR KEENING & REJOICING
OVER THE COMING END ...

TIME NOW TO FACE OUTWARD
IN THE FULL LOTUS POSITION
WITH EYES WIDE OPEN,

TIME NOW TO OPEN YOUR MOUTHS
WITH A NEW OPEN SPEECH,
TIME NOW TO COMMUNICATE WITH ALL
SENTIENT BEINGS ...

ALL YOU EYELESS UNREALISTS,
ALL YOU SELF-OCCULTING
SUPERSURREALISTS,
ALL YOU BEDROOM VISIONARIES
AND CLOSET AGITPROPAGATORS ...

WHERE THE GREAT VOICES SPEAKING OUT
WITH A SENSE OF SWEETNESS AND
SUBLIMITY,
WHERE THE GREAT'NEW VISION,
THE GREAT WORLD-VIEW,

THE HIGH PROPHETIC SONG
OF THE IMMENSE EARTH
AND ALL THAT SINGS IN IT
AND OUR RELATIONS TO IT ...

POETS, DESCEND
TO THE STREET OF THE WORLD ONCE MORE
AND OPEN YOUR MINDS & EYES
WITH THE OLD VISUAL DELIGHT,
CLEAR YOUR THROAT AND SPEAK UP ...

DON'T WAIT FOR THE REVOLUTION
OR IT'LL HAPPEN WITHOUT YOU,
STOP MUMBLING AND SPEAK OUT ...

THEY HAVEN'T PUT UP THE BARRICADES, YET,
THE STREETS STILL ALIVE WITH FACES,
LOVELY MEN & WOMEN STILL WALKING THERE,
STILL LOVELY CREATURES EVERYWHERE,

IN THE EYES OF ALL THE SECRET OF ALL
STILL BURIED THERE,
WHITMAN'S WILD CHILDREN STILL SLEEPING THERE,
AWAKE AND WALK IN THE OPEN AIR.
- LAWRENCE FERLINGHETTI

A Better Answer

There is a better answer to *the systemic problems of the system ...* one that doesn't favor of Wall Street so heavily. The better answer is a banking system that is not exclusively debt based and where no bank is "too big to fail." With a better answer, the government will never again be on the hook for trillions of dollars in bailouts and guarantees. This new system will value what we need as a society to create a sustainable, equitable and economically stable future for all without rewarding the speculation and creation of phantom wealth that has become the norm on Wall Street. The better answer will value the contributions of ordinary citizens– commitment, community, caring, and sustainability. The better answer to will democratize and decentralize the power to create money. This simple shift in thinking will change everything and inspire hope for millions of Americans who now despair of their economic future.

The severity of our current crises can serve as a wake up call. Suddenly the magnitude of the challenges that await us have come into bold relief. This will force us to think is a new way about long term sustainable solutions. For those with uncommon vision, a new path is emerging – a new way to address the root cause of our economic crisis. To understand this better I invite you to read the other books in this series:

- ***Main Street Versus Wall Street:*** *Transforming Raw Anger Into Purposeful Action*
- ***Meaningful Money:*** *Innovation at the Intersection of Money, Meaning and Markets*
- ***Common Cents:*** *New Money Versus Old Money and the Next American Revolution*
- ***The Wiz of Iz:*** *A Prophesy About the Coming Revolution*

About the Author - John F. Ince

John F. Ince is an author, social entrepreneur, journalist, blogger, podcaster, video producer, photographer and documentary filmmaker. He is founder / CEO of The Credit Commons and  Moneeey, Inc.. He previously worked as a reporter for *Fortune Magazine,* as a contributing editor with *Upside Magazine* and as a casewriter at Harvard Business School and Harvard's John F. Kennedy School of Government. Before that he worked for Sea Pines Company and on Wall Street with Chase Manhattan Bank. He served as an aide to former Senator Paul Tsongas organizing a U.S. Senate caucus for solar energy. He has founded two non profits, One World Inc. and The Earth Aid Foundation. He is the author of The Earth Pledge and organized the Earth Pledge Campaign in conjunction with the 25th anniversary celebration of Earth Day. He is an honors graduate of Harvard College where he was First Marshal (President) of his graduating class. He received his MBA from Harvard Business School in Finance.

For those interested in learning more about how the ideas presented in this book will work in practice, please read John Ince's other books in this series:

A Prophesy About the Coming Revolution

Two years ago, anticipating the coalescence of a movement that today is taking the form of Occupy Wall Street, I let my imagination take me into the future and penned, a somewhat whimsical and, it turns out, quite prophetic work of fiction: *The Wiz of Iz: a Prophesy About the Coming Revolution*. That book is about an inchoate movement led by a metaphorical leader who represents hope for change.... and the movement grows virally using modern technology. The book is also about the role of technology layered upon widespread popular discontent with the status quo of economic inequality.

The Wiz of Iz is a prophesy in the form of a powerful parable – a story where the characters represent something much more than who they are. The Wiz of Iz is a modern day version of *The Wizard of Oz*, a story many believe was written as a parable about the world of money and banking?

We're now living through an epochal period of change, though most people are too busy to realize what's really going on. We need to understand the root causes of these changes and we need vehicle to invite participation in ways that are peaceful, creative, non threatening - even playful. The tactics of the Occupy Movement have some of these characteristics.

The world is at an inflection point in history and we need to understand what's really happening to the culture and institutions that influence our lives. We need a common story to help understand what we're all going through. The Wiz of Iz contains a powerful truth in the form of a big idea. This idea, like a philosophers stone, must be viewed from different angles to behold it in all its splendor. This idea is seen from diverse perspectives through the prism of the Ten Traces of Truth inscribed on the Tablet of Truth. It relates to the most powerful tool ever created by humans–MONEY.

Today the meaning of money is finding its way into the our economic equation with the blending of emerging trends like social enterprise, social media, clean technology, slow money, free banking, virtual currency, cybercash, mobile payments, renewable energy, venture philanthropy, micro-finance, complementary currencies, green marketing, socially responsible investing and other trends that have not yet been labeled. Most of these ideas still operate at the periphery of our economy, but they're moving towards the mainstream.

Yet even as these emerging values grow in significance, they have not yet been ingrained into the code of money itself. That moment is fast approaching and when it happens, this movement will move into the forefront of our consciousness. It's an inevitable stage in the ongoing evolution of money and money systems. The code we program into the design of our money and our money systems is the strongest motivational force ever devised by humans. Money holds a mysterious power over our lives - a power so great it either push entire nations to the brink of collapse or inspire an their economic awakening. It can concentrate financial power in a few hands or democratize economic power. It can create new waves of wealth creation benefitting all of society or cause convulsions of economic instability that cause pain for everyone. It can stimulate prosperity or cause a contraction of business. It can raise hopes or dash dreams.

Modern technology today offers us amazing new possibilities in the way we create, use and share our money. The key to unlocking the higher potential of money is new thinking about a new kind money–a more Meaningful Money that incorporates a new consciousness that might be called the Code of Common Cents.

We need a story that proffers insight into the nature of the crisis we're going through and enables us to draw something powerful out of the depths of our collective soul. In times of economic crisis, and there is a real need for the uplift of bold new ideas, but change won't come from use smoke and mirrors to mask real problems. It won't come from quick fixes, used to avoid long term problems. Genuine change only comes when we advance our thinking into new and more fertile fields of discussion: fields where value and values are merged in new kind of marketplace.

The plot of *The Wiz of Iz* roughly follows the plot of The Wizard of Oz. A cast of allegorical figures from The Land of Iz, find themselves lost in a land of negativity called The Land of Izn't controlled by the Deputies of the Demon of Darkness. These intrepid souls want to return to their Land of Iz, but are told that they must first find Ten Truths which taken together constitute the Tablet of Truth. These characters follow the Rainbow Road where they meet elders, experts and eccentrics, who each provide a trace of truth which must be piece together into the Tablet of Truth before the Switch of Significance can be flipped and a Common Cents Code embedded into the Meaningful Money System. will take hold. Each in their own way is seeking empowerment to contend with the crises they face. They too hope that The Wiz of Iz can help them "flip the Switch of Significance" to create change we need. Sound familiar? All this, of course, is a literary vehicle for exploring the future dimensions of our current economic, environmental, spiritual and social crises in a way that invites reader enjoyment without burden of heavy ideas and dense economic theories. Author's Preface

We're in the midst of historic economic, political and ecological crises. We need to at least consider the possibility that these crises stem from systemic flaws that will require systemic solutions. In *The Wiz of Iz*, I included a new Declaration of Independence, adapted from the original by just changing a few words. It's really quite amazing how timely that document is today more that 200 years after it was written.

A revolution is coming and … it's just Common Cents.

The Declaration of Independence From The Demon of Darkness*

*Represents Unrestrained Corporate Power

Adapted from the original text of the Declaration of Independence by The Wiz of Iz

Adopted by the Unanimous Declaration of The Insurgents of Iz

When, in the course of human events, it becomes necessary for the people to adjust the economic binds which have connected them with the oppressive systems of the Demon of Darkness, and to assume among the powers of the people, the ability to build separate and equal operating systems to which the laws of nature and of nature's God entitle them, a decent respect to the opinions of mankind requires that they should declare the causes which impel them to the change the existing code of the operating system for the economy.

We hold these truths to be self-evident, that all men and women are created with equal economic opportunity, that they are endowed by their Creator with certain unalienable rights, that among these are life, financial liberty and the pursuit of economic happiness. That to secure these rights, operating systems for the global economy are instituted among men and women, deriving their just economic powers from the consent and cooperation of the common citizens. That whenever any form of operating system becomes destructive to these ends, it is the right of the people to withdraw their support, and to write a new Code of Common Cents, laying its foundation on such principles and organizing newer, and more equitable systems in such form, as to them shall seem most likely to effect their financial safety and economic happiness.

Prudence, indeed, will dictate that code of the global operating system, long established should not be changed for light and transient causes; and accordingly all experience hath shown that humans are more disposed to suffer, while evils are sufferable, than to right themselves by altering the forms to which they are accustomed. But when a long train of abuses and usurpations, pursuing invariably the same objective of economic advantage and unjust financial gain, evinces a design to reduce them under absolute economic despotism, it is their right, it is their duty, to alter such code, and to program a new code that guards their future economic security.

Such has been the patient sufferance of the citizens of the land; and such is now the necessity which constrains them to alter the code of existing systems. The history of the financial oppression of the Demon of Darkness is a history of repeated economic injuries and economic usurpations, all having in direct object the establishment of economic injustice. To prove this, let facts about the operators of these oppressive financial systems be submitted to a candid world.

• They have refused their assent to laws, the most wholesome and necessary for the public good.
• They have lobbied legislatures to pass laws creating immediate and pressing advantage for their operations.
• They have refused to accommodate their customers and clients, unless those people would pay exorbitant interest rates and excessive fees hidden in the fine print tyrannical agreements.
• They have called together legislators at places of unusual luxury and comfort, for the sole purpose of plying them with favors and campaign contributions seeking to entice them into compliance with their measures.
• They have intimidated elected representatives and government regulators repeatedly, for opposing with manly firmness their invasions on the unjust advantages of their station.
• They have refused for a long time, to return to the people at large the economic power to which they are entitled; the government remaining in the meantime exposed to all the economic dangers of financial crisis from foreign creditors, and convulsions within.
• They have endeavored to restrict credit allocation to the people of the land; for that purpose obstructing the free flow of capital for their own selfish purposes of financial appropriation of government issued bailout funds.
• They have obstructed the administration of justice by refusing to assent to laws for establishing regulatory powers.
• They have made elected officials dependent on their will, for the tenure of their offices, and the amount and payment of campaign contributions.
• They have erected a multitude of new artifices, and sent hither swarms of self serving experts, armed with manufactured arguments, press releases and

distortions of fact, to manipulate public opinion, and eat away at the substance of truth.

• They have kept among us, in times of financial crisis, standing armies of financial engineers, number crunchers and wily persuaders in order to win the consent of our legislature for government bailouts towards their own selfish financial ends.

• They have affected to render the their own political powers independent of and superior to the power of the citizens.

• They have combined with others to subject us to a jurisdiction foreign sources of capital that places foreign creditors in a superior position to the citizens of the nation and our elected representatives.

We have warned them from time to time of attempts by their legislature to extend an unwarrantable jurisdiction over us. We have reminded them of the circumstances of our emigration and settlement here. We have appealed to their native justice and magnanimity, and we have conjured them by the ties of our common kindred to disavow these usurpations, which, would inevitably interrupt our connections and correspondence. They too have been deaf to the voice of justice and of consanguinity.

We, therefore, the people of the Land of Iz, do solemnly publish and declare, that these united people are, and of right ought to be free and independent of these economic oppressors; and that as free and independent people, we have full power to create new Common Cents Code that will establish our own economic independence.

And for the support of this declaration, with a firm reliance on The Wiz of Iz, we mutually pledge to each other our lives, our Meaningful Moneeey and our sacred honor.

MAIN STREET
VERSUS
WALL STREET

How We Can Fix
A Broken System

JOHN F. INCE

COMMON CENTS

CENTS

NEW MONEY VS OLD MONEY
AND THE NEXT AMERICAN
REVOLUTION

JOHN F. INCE

Meaningful
MONEY

INNOVATION AT THE
INTERSECTION OF ...

MONEY, MEANING
AND MARKETS

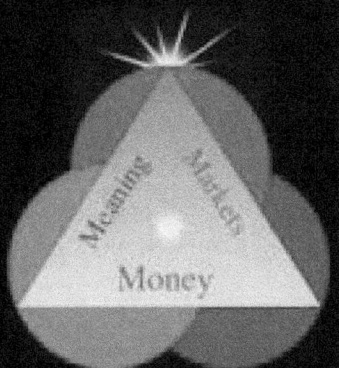

JOHN F. INCE

***

TO JOIN WITH OTHERS CONCERNED ABOUT
GENERAL ISSUES
RAISED IN THIS BOOK VISIT:
WWW.WSVMS.NET

TO JOIN A CONVERSATION ABOUT THE CREDIT
COMMONS VISIT:
WWW. WSVMS.NET

TO ASK QUESTIONS OF THE AUTHOR EMAIL:
JINCE@WSVMS.COM

FOR ADDITIONAL COPIES OF THIS BOOK VISIT:
WWW. WSVMS.COM

TO READ JOHN F. INCE'S BLOG VISIT:
WWW. JOHNINCE.COM

TO FOLLOW JOHN INCE ON TWITTER VISIT:
HTTP://TWITTER.COM/JOHNINCE

FOR ADDITIONAL INFORMATION OR
FOR DISCOUNTS ON BULK ORDERS OF THIS
BOOK EMAIL:

INFO@ WSVMS.COM

***